Writing the City

LALH

Writing the City

ESSAYS ON NEW YORK

ELIZABETH BARLOW ROGERS

Library of American Landscape History

Amherst, Massachusetts

Library of American Landscape History
P.O. Box 1323
Amherst, MA 01004
www.lalh.org

Printed in the United States of America by Porter Print Group, LLC

Library of Congress Control Number: 2021947106
ISBN: 978-1-952620-36-2

Designed by Jonathan D. Lippincott
Set in Sabon

Distributed by
National Book Network
nbnbooks.com

Publication of *Writing the City* is supported by the Nancy R. Turner Fund.

For both native and adopted New Yorkers
who call this city their home of the heart

Contents

Preface

As author, historian, and founder of the Central Park Conservancy, Elizabeth Barlow Rogers's contributions to cultural landscape studies and preservation practice have influenced scholarship internationally and catalyzed the restoration of landscapes worldwide. Her magnum opus, *Landscape Design: A Cultural and Architectural History*, one of eleven books she has published, was a singular gift to the field of landscape studies—and to intellectual and cultural history generally

Without question, Rogers ranks as the patron saint of New York's most famous park, which has been the subject of several of her essays and books. In the new LALH volume, *Writing the City*, she trains her cultural historian's eye on a wide range of places across the boroughs, focusing on them from bold and unusual perspectives. Written over four decades of living and working in New York, these essays capture her insights about many of the city's most important landscapes as they have been shaped through the centuries by the people who lived there and by the forces of nature before humankind ever came to inhabit the region.

Reading Rogers's essays in the order they appear provides a deep dive into the evolution of the city. She is a deft interpreter of natural history, and her introductory account of the city's ancient geological history—beginning 700 million years ago—is riveting. Her second essay, "A Once and Future Arcadia," includes observations

from Dutch settlers delighted by the bounty of the land and sweet-
ness of the air. She also includes musings by Dickens, who visited
in 1842, by which time slums were proliferating. "Debauchery has
made the very houses prematurely old," he observed of one neighborhood. "See how the rotten beams are tumbling down, and how
the patched and broken windows seem to scowl dimly, like eyes that
have been hurt in drunken frays."

As the city began its long struggle with urban decay, the Hudson River of the mid-nineteenth century retained its bucolic aspect.
Rogers traces the history of the early Dutch farmers who settled its
banks and also quotes the Swedish naturalist Peter Kalm, who in
1792 wrote delightedly of watching porpoises "play and tumble"
in the river. In time, the Hudson's extraordinary beauty drew artists and writers, including William Cullen Bryant, who found the
western shore of the Hudson "as worthy of a pilgrimage across the
Atlantic as the Alps themselves." Written in 1972, seven agoniz-
ing years before Con Ed relinquished plans to build a power plant
on Storm King Mountain, Rogers's essay also conveys pessimism
about the future. "Yet," she concludes, "it would be premature to
write the obituary of the Hudson. The river itself still lives, its powerful current alternating direction with the tides."

Among the designed landscapes Rogers discusses is the New
York Botanical Garden. The list of protagonists in this complex
story features NYBG's first director, Nathaniel Britton, and his
wife Elizabeth, an accomplished bryologist (a botanist specializing
in liverworts and mosses), who cofounded the remarkable institution in 1891. Rogers's account includes as well others better known
today, such as the landscape architects Marian Coffin, Ellen Shipman, and Beatrix Farrand, all of whom designed gardens for its
250 acres. (In 1915, Farrand imaginatively suggested getting cost
estimates for individual sections of her rose garden, "so that they
could be tabulated and dangled before prospective subscribers"—a
foreshadowing of Rogers's own fundraising strategies as president
of the Central Park Conservancy, the subject of a later essay in this
collection).

Rogers's deep understanding of landscape design is on full display in "Beneath the Great Bridge," an account of the first years of planning Brooklyn Bridge Park. Written in 2001, before construction began, the essay explains the principles underlying Michael Van Valkenburgh's brilliant design, including his rubric of four landscape types: natural, boundless, civic, and urban. Here Rogers presciently predicts the success of Van Valkenburgh's visionary techniques, which resulted in one of the great urban waterfront parks of the twentieth century.

A previously unpublished essay on Prospect Park situates Olmsted and Vaux's remarkable design in relation to Central Park. Rogers offers insight into the drama surrounding Olmsted's reluctant decision to undertake the 1866 commission in Brooklyn—and Calvert Vaux's pivotal role in catalyzing it. Unfettered by the gridded street patterns of Manhattan, the landscape architects were able to achieve a more expansive pastoral design in the still-unsettled site. Facing similar preservation challenges to those Rogers confronted at Central Park, Tupper Thomas, Prospect Park administrator, is here celebrated for her leadership in the remarkably successful campaign she led to recover its original beauty.

No one has taken New York City Park Commissioner Robert Moses to task with more incisiveness than Rogers. She follows Moses from the 1930s, as he constructs popular but scenically intrusive recreational facilities throughout Central Park, to his Waterloo moment in 1960, when he took steps to construct a large modernist building, a café that would seat five hundred people on each of its two levels, at the park's southeast corner. She gives the last word to Tiffany & Company CEO Walter Hoving, who had filed a lawsuit to stop the project. "Some officials in office a long time seem to get a sovereignty complex. Not only do they feel they know better than the rest of us taxpayers, but they ride roughshod . . . notably Robert Moses, whose . . . habitual arrogance, particularly in this situation, I decry."

The inclusion in this collection of "Thirty-three New Ways You Can Help Central Park's Renaissance" illuminates a specific moment in the rebirth of the park—1983—when much had been accomplished, but much remained to be done to fulfill the Conservancy's management plan. Published as a follow-up to a similar *New York* magazine piece that ran in 1976, Rogers's list is notable for its sophistication and foresight: computerized tree inventory, intern training, wildflower meadows, archival photograph reproduction, a new "radio command center," and soil enrichment. There were more modest projects on offer, too, including restoring a park bench (for $30.80—replacement slats cost $3.85 apiece) and new trash barrels at $32.50.

In "Jane and Me," the concluding essay in this collection, Rogers distinguishes her own perspectives on city planning from those of Jane Jacobs, whose *Death and Life of Great American Cities* first inspired Rogers to seek a master's degree in the subject from Yale. Jacobs concurred with then-popular opinion that parks should not be built in urban areas associated with "down-and-outers," and she also "frowned upon siting parks in commercial districts because these locations did not encourage sociable recreational use." Experience has taught—and Rogers figures among our most able teachers—that urban parks work their magic in a great range of settings throughout a city. We see the wisdom of this perspective, especially in New York, where Rogers's impact has been transformative.

Funding for *Writing the City* came from the Nancy R. Turner Fund and from Cynthia Hewitt and Dan Holloway, to whom we are deeply grateful. We are also grateful to Sara Cedar Miller and the Central Park Conservancy for use of the beautiful photographs on the jacket.

Robin Karson, Hon. ASLA
Executive Director
LALH

Writing the City

Introduction

On my daily walks in Central Park I often pause to read the inscriptions on the bench plaques. Some memorialize departed family members, others serve as valentines in bronze celebrating couples' love, and many pay tribute to the park itself as someone's place of the heart. The dedication that caught my eye today reads:

> *For Ann Owen*
> *A Southerner who loves*
> *The people, culture, and parks of New York*

I have never met Ann Owen, but I hope that someday I will have a chance to shake her hand and say, "Me too!"

I grew up in San Antonio, Texas, but New York City has been my ardently adopted home for over half a century. That I was imprinted so decisively by my association with the people, culture, and parks of New York is apparent in the way I appropriated as mine "this mischievous and marvelous monument which not to look upon would be like death," as the Pulitzer Prize–winning journalist E. B. White put it in the final sentence of his 1949 classic paean to the city, *Here Is New York.*

Writing about a love affair, as White did in his essay-length book and the affectionate Talk of the Town pieces he wrote during his many years as a regular contributor to the *New Yorker,* is one of the ways a person forges her own identity with place. My love affair has been conducted, as was White's, through literary endeavors. Less psychologically descriptive and more fact-focused than his evocative tribute, the magazine articles, journal essays, and public speeches I have gathered in this volume are evidence of this. Organized under three topical rubrics, my book is also written from the heart—in my case, the heart of an urban explorer and landscape historian.

·

Part I, "Below and Above the Ground," debunks the common perception that the words "nature" and "city" are contradictory, especially when the city is a great metropolis. The course of my life, and a good deal of my writer's capital, are the result of personal discovery of the city's natural endowment, together with the elements of nature fostered within it by landscape designers and urban gardeners. A related part of my self-education has been derived from the collections, exhibitions, publications, and programs offered by two of the city's great cultural institutions—the New York Botanical Garden and the American Museum of Natural History—ideal destinations for students of the relationships between art and nature.

The first essay explores the city's physical fundament, its underlying geology, the genesis of its topography of rivers, bays, beaches, rocky ridges, salt marshes, meadows, and streams. Mantling much of this landscape were dense forests of oak, hickory, and chestnut, the subject of the second essay. More than three centuries before my own discovery of contemporary New York City as a fortunate place to put down roots, it was discovered by the European explorers who entered the Narrows, the tidal strait that forms the principal channel where the Hudson River empties into the ocean, making New York a port city with one of the finest harbors in the world. The native wonders they beheld with astonished and acquisitive eyes as they voyaged through its waters and viewed the peripheral landscape are discussed here.

The Hudson River itself has been the subject of many writers including me, as is evident in the third essay, an article I wrote for *New York* magazine in 1972. Here the story of the once busy thor-

oughfare of transportation and commerce banked by scenic mag-
nificence is treated in a then-and-now manner, recalling the time
when its clear waters fostered an abundance of marine life and
deploring their subsequent degradation by the release of polychlori-
nated biphenyl chemicals (PCBs) from nearby industrial plants and
other forms of environmental pollution that destroyed the breeding
and feeding grounds of striped bass, shad, and several other once
prolific aquatic species. Written in the early days of the environmental movement, the article's underlying message is the need to estab-
lish water cleanup and natural resources conservation as principled
political priorities. At the same time, it takes the reader on a tour of
some of the splendid mansions in the Hudson River Valley, including Frederic Church's Olana, a candidate for the kind of carefully
researched architectural restoration being proposed at the time by
recently chartered historic preservation organizations.

Since this section of the book is focused on natural history, I
have also included two essays I wrote more recently, one about the
landscape design history of the New York Botanical Garden and
the other about the creation of the American Museum of Natural
History's dioramas as an art form representing full-scale lifelike
native and exotic fauna.

·

Part II, "Along the Shoreline," contains my 2005 review of a book
composed of perceptive observations of the human side of Manhattan's shoreline, an account of the nascence of Brooklyn Bridge
Park in 2000, and the establishment of the South Street Seaport
Historical District in 1971. Consulting a map will help you put
these three articles into context. Trace the perimeters of Manhattan, Governors, and Staten Islands and the boundaries of the boroughs of Brooklyn, Queens, and the Bronx where they meet the
water. These are the shorelines of New York City—520 coastal
miles in all, spread along the Hudson, Harlem, and East Rivers,
the Narrows, Long Island Sound, and the Atlantic Ocean. If you
imagine yourself walking at the rate of 3.5 miles an hour for ten
hours a day, you can figure that it will take you two strenuous

weeks to see the city's shoreline up close in its entirety. Should you opt for a more likely one-day challenge, you can sign up for the annual Great Saunter organized by the Shorewalkers, a non-profit group founded in 1982. Usually held on the first Saturday in May, this thirty-two-mile Manhattan perimeter hike is a notable accomplishment that ranks with completing a New York City Marathon.

A peripatetic urban walker with a seasoned journalist's talent for social observation, the Brooklyn-born writer Phillip Lopate, who is best known for his anthology *The Art of the Personal Essay,* is himself a notable essayist. The first piece in this section is a review I wrote for the May 2005 issue of *The New Criterion* of Lopate's *Waterfront: A Journey around Manhattan.* In it I note that "the entire circuit that this walker in the city makes around Manhattan's waterfront, narrated as the story of one man's love affair with the greatest city on earth and the incomparable estuarine harbor that set its dynamic development in motion, is fascinating and timely."

No one who falls in love with New York, whether a native like Lopate or an immigrant like me, can fail to see the potential of the waterfront for the creation of linear public promenades and parks now that most of the piers from an earlier period in the city's life as a functioning port have become obsolete. As a park-focused urban planner, I have witnessed the extension to the south of Riverside Park, the renewal of historic Battery Park at the lower tip of Manhattan, the transformation of the abandoned elevated rail spur known as the High Line into a world-famous aerial promenade, and the conversion of the right-of-way of the old West Side Highway into Hudson River Park. I was also an interested follower of the political campaign for the creation of Brooklyn Bridge Park, beginning in the late 1990s with the formation of the Downtown Brooklyn Waterfront Local Development Corporation, which prepared a conceptual framework for a waterfront park on a three-mile stretch of the East River occupied by six defunct cargo shipping piers located beneath the Brooklyn Bridge. The second essay in this section is an article I wrote for

the Winter 2000–2001 issue of the *Cityscape News,* a publication
of the Cityscape Institute, a short-lived organization I founded in
1996 after I stepped down from the presidency of the Central Park
Conservancy.

Three decades earlier I had witnessed the beginning of the reclamation of another stretch of East River waterfront on the opposite bank from the new Brooklyn Bridge Park. I recapture this
experience in the next piece, an article I wrote for the August 1971
issue of *Smithsonian* magazine, "On New York's Aged Waterfront,
a Pinch of Salt." It recounts one man's vision for refurbishing some
of the old warehouse buildings at the foot of Fulton Street and the
creation of a maritime museum for the display of scrimshaw and
other artifacts from the days when the fictional Ahab captained
the whaling vessel *Pequod* in Melville's *Moby Dick.* In a handful of the remaining berths of the East River piers, the nascent
museum had also begun to dock six vintage vessels in the process
of being restored to their original state, most notably the towering
square-rigger *Wavertree.*

At the time I wrote the article you could imagine that you were
getting a faint whiff of the printers' ink that had once been sold
to the city's thriving newspaper businesses. I was told that as a
time-traveler I could have also smelled coffee being roasted and
leather tanned, all cheek-by-jowl operations in the row of narrow
brick establishments that were part of old South Street as an industrial zone before it was embalmed as a historic district bounded by
financial institutions to the west, southwest, and north, the East
River to the southeast, and the Manhattan and Brooklyn Bridges
to the northeast.

When I was visiting South Street doing research for my article in
1971, I would often buy a striped bass caught the same day from one
of the fishmongers in the still thriving Fulton Street Fish Market. If
it was noon and I was hungry, I would have lunch at Sloppy Louie's,
the fishermen's favorite eatery, which was immortalized by the *New
Yorker* writer Joseph Mitchell in his legendary 1952 article "Up in
the Old Hotel." For an evening dinner out on the town with friends
there was Sweet's, another fresh-from-the-dock seafood establish-

ment on Schermerhorn Row, which gained culinary fame during its 150 years in business until its closure in 1992.

In the process of funding the administration of the South Street Seaport as a city-designated historic district and museum, the vision of its founders to preserve an urban relic of maritime Manhattan morphed into an upscale restoration of the district as a tourist attraction with a trendy mall. The old industrial brick building that was once New York City's most famous fish market was radically renovated and, according to one current Google review, its recent remodeling has added "a hip vibe to it." Including my own vintage *Smithsonian* article about this piece of waterfront New York in this anthology is thus for me an act of nostalgia.

·

Part III, "In and About the Parks," begins in Brooklyn with a history of Green-Wood Cemetery, which might be called a proto-park when one considers it as an inspirational precursor of Central Park. Indeed, this catalyst for the late-1840s rural cemetery movement in America had become a venue for family outings as well as family burials, which fostered the campaign in the mid-1850s to build a great people's park in the center of Manhattan. At this time Brooklyn was still a self-governing municipality, and in 1865, with competitive civic zeal, a group of leading citizens commissioned Central Park's designers, Frederick Law Olmsted and Calvert Vaux, to create another masterpiece of Romantic naturalistic design, Prospect Park, the subject of the next essay.

After I founded the Central Park Conservancy in 1980, my writing skills were directed almost exclusively to the preparation of grant proposals, annual reports, letters to donors and members of the board, and speeches to citizen groups in several American cities who were forming park conservancies based on the Central Park model. My message in these public appearances was almost always the same. I said that I was opposed to a mere "fix-it" approach focused only on prominent park features; rather, I argued, there should be a holistic vision that encompassed these within an entire landscape framework. Such how-to advice included preaching the necessity for visionary leadership, a committed board of directors, and the preparation of a comprehensive, park-wide plan to fulfill the mission of these citizen-led public–private organizations.

My most important literary endeavor during this time was the publication of *Rebuilding Central Park: A Management and Restoration Plan* (MIT Press, 1987), the fruit of the efforts of the Conservancy's team of landscape architects and ancillary consultants to reestablish as much as possible of the badly neglected horticultural and arboricultural fabric and as many of the near-ruined architectural features of Olmsted and Vaux's original Greensward plan as possible. During the three years we worked toward this goal it became increasingly obvious that our task had a further dimension. The public-works czar Robert Moses, who also served as commissioner of New York City's parks department from 1934 until 1960, had thoroughly imprinted the park with facilities dedicated to active recreation. This was a direct contradiction of the principals behind the park's original Olmstedian design, which was intended for unprogrammed enjoyment of fresh air and views of naturalistic scenery by all classes of urban dwellers as opposed to prescribed play for single-purpose constituencies.

With no affinity for the aesthetics of landscape design as expressed in the park's original Greensward plan, Moses saw Central Park's 843 acres as merely a tabula rasa on which to impose his autocratic political will. Thus, immediately after he took office broad meadows were turned into ball fields, twenty-two playgrounds encircled by tall wrought-iron palings were installed near park entrances, rustic gazebos were torn down, and with the exception of the Dairy and the Belvedere, original park buildings were replaced with architecturally undistinguished ones designed in a uniform style to house comfort stations, park concessions, and maintenance and sports equipment. Park paths were paved with asphalt and lined with concrete curbing, and the shorelines of the Pond and Harlem Meer were banked with riprap. The complete story of how Moses transformed the design face and landscape fabric of Central Park, both for better and for worse, goes largely unrecognized, a lacuna I have filled in the third essay in this section, which first appeared in the Fall 2007 issue of the Foundation for Landscape Studies' journal *Site/Lines*.

Such a dispassionate historical narrative, written in hindsight, does not exonerate Moses but shows the role that sociological evolution plays in the nature of human activities and the elements of the built environment that support them. This was an important truth I had to learn since it would have been political folly as well as indifference to twentieth-century recreational preferences to uphold in its entirety the nineteenth-century designers' original intention of creating a green oasis for passive repose in the middle of the city. It was thus clear to me and the Conservancy's landscape restoration planning team that absolutely authentic historic landscape restoration of the park had its limits and that combining Olmstedian design principles with Moses's Central Park legacy was an essential prerequisite to popular success.

Large-scale fundraising was a necessity if the Central Park Conservancy were to execute its management and restoration plan. In order to accomplish this multiyear endeavor, publicity was important. Thus it was through writing that I began to develop my skills as a fundraiser. Fortunately, I was not entirely inexperienced in this regard. Five years before the birth of the Conservancy I had established the Central Park Task Force to run volunteer and summer-jobs-for-youth programs as well as educational activities for school students while at the same time undertaking a series of studies to enable the rehabilitation of the park's landscape and deteriorated architectural elements. Luckily, during the life of the Task Force I was commissioned to write an article titled "32 Ways Your Time or Money Can Rescue Central Park" for *New York* magazine, published in June 1976. Essentially a catalog of gift opportunities for such obvious remedies as controlling erosion on slopes, becoming a member of the "weed patrol," helping the police assigned to Central Park do a better job (a plea for volunteers to assist officers by joining the Bike Patrol, Medical Rescue, or Playground Watchers units), restoring shrub beds, and giving the Conservatory Garden as well as the Shakespeare Garden new horticultural leases on life.

The $25,000 that came in a week later, mostly in small denominations accompanied by letters filled with memories of childhoods, courtships, and parental experiences, plus a sheer love of Central Park even in its derelict state, gave me the confidence that the citizens of New York were willing to support the possibility of remedy. Once the Conservancy had been formed and its management and restoration plan was being successfully implemented, *New York* again gave me a platform to broadcast the message that Central Park could be restored to its former beauty and good maintenance through the support of private citizens. This time I was able to offer prospective donors a section-by-section selection of projects throughout the entire park that would, like a completed jigsaw puzzle, form an integrated whole.

Compared with the earlier *New York* article, this one from June 1983, which is republished here as the fourth essay in Part III, calls for the funding of park maintenance projects of greater magnitude, since by this time we had established crews for graffiti removal, bronze and stone sculpture conservation, turf care, tree pruning, shrub and flower planting, construction of rustic structures, masonry repointing, and carpentry repairs, while also instituting the hiring of zone gardeners with accountability for the cleanliness and horticultural care of defined sections of the park.

Much as Frederick Law Olmsted was a guiding star in my firmament of professional inspiration and Robert Moses a force with which to reckon, Jane Jacobs was my urban planning hero. Her 1961 book *The Death and Life of Great American Cities* was effectively a diatribe against modernist master planning in the mold of Moses. His penchant for building highways and replacing socially close-woven ethnic neighborhoods with urban renewal housing projects were Jacobs's twin bêtes noires. Although her vision of urban planning as a means of salvaging a city's own socially vibrant past by preserving old neighborhoods did not go down well with my professors during the 1960s when I was a graduate student in the Yale School of City Planning, my allegiance to the views Jacobs espoused was instrumental in fostering my predilection for people-friendly open-space creation and conservation rather than the transformation of cities according to the planning principles of such theorists of radical modernity as Le Corbusier. The story of this life-changing attitude on my part is recounted in the final piece in this collection, the text of a speech I gave in June 2016 as part of the Jane Jacobs Centennial Lecture Series organized by Roberta Gratz.

•

As someone who looks on urban planning as an important part of landscape history, I was pleased when I was asked by Robin Karson, the founder and executive director of the Library of American Landscape History, to assemble this collection of my writings on New York City spanning my career as an environmentalist, historic landscape preservationist, and writer on the subject of place.

This afternoon, when I had finished selecting the pieces collected here, I decided to take a walk in Central Park. It was a cold, somewhat windy, and intermittently rainy afternoon, so I moved briskly while still glancing at the messages on the plaques of the benches encircling the Great Lawn. On the opposite side of the Lawn from the spot where I had first made note of the one anonymously donated in honor of Ann Owen, I paused to put up my umbrella. Looking down, I saw an inscription that perfectly fit the weather and my current mood. The words, which had been chosen by another anonymous donor, read "Even a bad day in Central Park is better than a good day anywhere else." "So true," I mentally agreed.

What words would I want to have inscribed on a bench plaque of my own, I wondered. This was not a question that was hard for me to answer: "Even a normal day in New York is better than an extraordinary day in any other city on earth." The magazine articles, essays, and speeches dating from 1971 to 2016 that make up this book are tributes to this urban wonder, with its fascinating natural history, scenic shorefront, and masterfully designed parks. The spirit in which they were written testifies that for me New York City is truly the home of the heart.

PART I

Below and Above the Ground

Bedrock, Sand, and Water

The Geological Landscape of New York City

(2013)

Sometimes I am asked what my favorite place in Central Park is, a question to which there is really no answer. The park is about circuitous movement through a sequence of scenes orchestrated by its designers, Frederick Law Olmsted and Calvert Vaux. The modeling of the park's terrain into gently swelling hills and broad, flat meadows; the creation of its naturalistic lakes, streams, and ponds; and the construction of its innovative circulation infrastructure of sunken transverse roads, interior carriage drives, pathways, and bridle trails, all of which are grade-separated for safety and convenience, provide an unparalleled demonstration of nineteenth-century engineering technology put in the service of a naturalistic landscape ideal.

But not all of Central Park is man-made. Nature played a singular role, too, one that Olmsted and Vaux were wise enough to take into account. The ingenuity of their plan, with its imaginative orchestration of scenically varied parts, capitalizes on a powerful natural feature: bold outcrops of Manhattan schist bedrock. Elsewhere, outside the park, bedrock protrusions were blasted away to make the ground plane an almost level surface in order to accommodate a grid of streets and avenues; within the park, however, selected rock outcrops were treated as important design elements.

From *Site/Lines* 9.1 (Fall 2013).

I love these great elephantine presences in the landscape. Some define the shoreline of the Lake; others guide the alignment of a path or provide a vantage point for viewing the surrounding park— as names such as Vista Rock and Summit Rock suggest. In addition, the glacially polished Manhattan schist outcrops in Central Park have smooth surfaces and easy footholds, which make them easy to climb. Olmsted and Vaux, moreover, catered to this urge by cutting steps into some of their surfaces. It is wonderful, really, to claim the top of one of these rock formations for relaxation and stretch out for a nap in the sun with exposed flesh touching warm stone.

Thus are these bold examples of local geology tamed by comfortable familiarity. They are our rocks—rooted, immovable, and unchanging in their mass and outlines. But are they? From a less personal perspective in which time is measured by Earth's own clock rather than our purely historical one based on the calendrical computation of dates they tell a story as fantastic as science fiction, only it deals not with the future but a past so extensive as to seem inconceivable to anyone other than an earth scientist. The following topographical narrative traces the origins of the place on the globe that became New York City.

Deep Time, Deep History

Long before New York became real estate, divided and occupied in accordance with political and economic dictates; long before it became imprinted with human occupation; in fact, long before the human species even existed, there were the land and the sea. And just as the New York of real estate and urban planning is dynamic— a city constantly erasing and rebuilding itself—the New York of bedrock, sand, and water is mobile and forever altering in response to the forces of geology and climate. Because it is difficult for us to realize from the perspective of our own short lifetimes that the only real permanence is change, we instinctively resist belief that Earth is anything but fixed in its place in the universe and that its geography is perpetually mutable. To project this scientific verity to a contemporary and local level, we must imagine the 1,792-foot-tall Freedom Tower at the former World Trade Center site drowned at some future date beneath hundreds of feet of seawater.

.

The latest geographical configuration of New York City, the five-borough one made up of the islands and mainland we know at present, is essentially the product of two forces. The first was an ancient tectonic event known as the Taconic orogeny, when the North American crustal plate was folded and deformed by lateral compression some 495 to 440 million years ago as the Iapetus Ocean, the precursor of the Atlantic, shrank during the collision of the North American continental plate and the neighboring oceanic plate. With the subduction of the latter as it moved sideways and downward beneath the earth's mantle, the folding and elevation of the eastern portion of the North American landmass occurred, giving birth to what are now the Appalachian Mountains. Eons of erosion caused their towering peaks to disappear until the continent's crustal subsurface was squeezed and uplifted once more by another tectonic episode, the Acadian orogeny, occurring between approximately 375 and 325 million years ago.

A much more recent landscape transformation occurred during the Late Pleistocene epoch, when a series of ice ages ensued. The last of these took place during the Wisconsin glaciation, 85,000 to 11,000 years ago, when a wall of ice approximately two miles in height covered what are now Canada and the northern United States. This ponderous moving force, with its load of rocks, gravel, and other abrasive debris, scoured and polished the eroded stumps of the ancient mountain range. Think about this when you are stretched out or sitting on your favorite rock in Central Park: you are, geologically speaking, deep underground in what was once the subsurface of a lofty mountain peak. Equally astonishing, a little more than ten thousand years ago your spot in the sun lay buried beneath a thousand feet of ice.

The face of Central Park, of course, is not the only one in New York City upon which to trace Earth's history firsthand. There are several other large parks that are exceptionally well endowed with evidence of the dynamic forces that account for the configuration of their current landscapes. Mine is a very partial and site-specific knowledge of geology, gleaned mainly from exploration of a handful of these unbuilt urban places—in particular, Inwood Hill Park, Pelham Bay Park, and the Staten Island Greenbelt—with Sidney Horenstein, a geologist at the American Museum of Natural History, and Michael Feller, the chief naturalist at the city's parks department. Here are some of the things I have learned from them.

New York City Geology 101

Seven hundred million years ago, the piece of geography now occupied by New York City lay far below sea level, accumulating sediments of mud and seawater precipitates of shale and limestone that were subsequently metamorphosed by heat from the interior mantle below Earth's crust to become strata of gneiss and marble. Then, some 300 million years later, during the Taconic orogeny, the pressure and intense heat produced by continental drift and the collision of two lithospheric plates turned these once solid strata, which had subsided under the weight of thousands of feet of subsequent sedimentation, into a mobile crustal mass capable of mineral transformation. Over more millions of years—again we are talking about what is to most of us an incomprehensible time scale—the mineral content of these original sedimentary strata changed as their ions reordered and recrystallized, hardening into much tougher, more coarsely grained formations as they reached a new and thermodynamically stable equilibrium. During this process the malleable material was slowly shoved into mountain-building folds.

Because of their mineral transformation, such rock formations are called metamorphic and given names other than those of their parent sedimentary strata. For example—to choose the rocks principally composing New York City—metamorphosed shale becomes either gneiss or schist, whereas limestone turns into marble.

Around 120 million years after the Taconic orogeny, the Acadian orogeny further metamorphosed formations whose minerals could still be traced to their parent sedimentary layers. The earth's intense internal pressure caused these formations to fracture. This allowed magma, molten material of igneous origin, to penetrate and separate the existing bedrock thereby creating a fault—a place where the earth's crust had fractured and slipped, creating a displacement and discontinuity between two strata. After it has cooled, crystallized, and solidified, a vertical igneous rock is called a dike. On the other hand, when created within a fracture cutting more or less horizontally across strata, the same rock is called a sill. For instance, the New Jersey Palisades is a sill, a solid wall whose tough igneous stone confines the west bank of the Hudson River. On a smaller scale, mineral intrusions derived from igneous material appear as bands or contorted strips that have been squeezed into fissures and cracks of older rocks.

Not surprisingly, mineralogists find New York City an optimal ground for study. Their extensive excavations of its bedrock have yielded over 170 of the earth's 2,000 known minerals, many of spectacular size and quite a few of gem quality. Amateur geologists who visit the city's parks and other places where there are exposed rock faces sometimes find granite pegmatites (a coarse-grained, crystalline granite with large mineral grains indicative of a slow cooling process) that are studded with garnets, tourmalines, beryls, and other semiprecious gemstones. Another igneous rock, serpentine, forms the hilly spine running down the center of Staten Island. Capping this ridge is Todt Hill, 410 feet above sea level, the highest landmark along the entire eastern coastline south of Massachusetts. This serpentine, like the metamorphic rocks discussed below, has undergone alteration far below the earth's surface. Unlike them, however, it was formed of igneous rather than sedimentary material.

The Big Three

New York City's most ubiquitous geological formations are three metamorphic ones: Fordham gneiss, Inwood marble, and Manhattan schist. The most ancient of these bedrock strata is the Fordham gneiss, an extremely contorted, metamorphosed sandstone characterized by wavy black-and-white bands. This is the primary underlying bedrock of the New York City area. Surface exposures of it appear mainly in the Bronx, notably in the New York Botanical Garden. A durable stone resistant to erosion, it forms an elevated ridge in Riverdale. The names Fordham Heights, Morris Heights, and Highbridge signify another prominent elevation of gneiss immediately to the east, where a two-pronged ridge is found. This formation slopes downward into the earth at a southeasterly angle, making its final surface appearance in Astoria, Queens.

Roosevelt Island in the East River is a spit of Fordham gneiss, too. Its stone—quarried by convict labor in the nineteenth century when the place was still known as Blackwell's Island—was used to build not only the island's almshouse but also a now-demolished gray, fortresslike prison and some of the hospitals in which the mentally ill and patients with infectious diseases were incarcerated.

The rock formation lying immediately above the Fordham gneiss is called Inwood marble. It takes its name from the Inwood section of Manhattan where it can be seen in a few exposed surfaces. Because marble is a soft stone, it is easily eroded. It is natural therefore that the Harlem and Hudson Rivers cut their beds into this formation rather than through the more resistant neighboring gneiss. The northeastern section of Manhattan upon which Harlem was built is also underlain with Inwood marble, as are parts of the Bronx. In colonial times, large portions of these flat, low-lying areas were covered with extensive salt marshes. In several places, long, continuous bands of Inwood marble lie between "heights" of tougher, less erosion-prone stone. These marble valleys were the most accessible transportation routes in the city's early days, and in time became its major thoroughfares. Broadway in Manhattan and its continuation in the Bronx, along with Jerome, Webster, and Tremont Avenues, also in the Bronx, are underlain with this soft, whitish stone.

The youngest formation is called Manhattan schist, often referred to as Manhattan mica schist because of the "books" of

mica, as their pagelike shiny mineral flecks often appear on the surface of Manhattan's schist outcrops, which were used as integral
elements in the design and building of Central Park. Less conspicuous, subterranean Manhattan schist is the bedrock that supports
the city's towering skyscrapers. For this reason, the division of the
island into two zones of tall buildings—downtown and midtown—
is not accidental. South of 30th Street, the bedrock dips several feet
beneath the earth but is still accessible for building foundations until
it reaches the north side of Washington Square, where it plunges
more than a hundred feet below the surface. Greenwich Village
and the loft district to the south form the "valley," a region of low
buildings set on top of glacial sediments and artificial landfill. Near
Chambers Street, however, the schist comes back to within fewer
than a hundred feet of street level to firmly anchor the towers of the
financial district. The zoning code of Manhattan is thus written as
much by geology as by city planners.

During the eons that these bedrock strata still lay within the
subterranean bowels beneath the earth's surface, their compression
and consequent subduction and upheaval along the easterly part of
the North American plate caused the formation of the 2000-mile
Appalachian mountain range. As their peaks eroded over time, the
ancient mountains responded by rising slowly. During the following multi-millenary periods of geological time they became layered
with additional sedimentary deposits. Subsequent earth movements
folded and pushed these into mountainous ridges and fractured the
old metamorphic formations beneath them, creating fault zones.
Once more all the sedimentary strata were almost entirely eroded,
leaving only the ancient metamorphic gneiss and marble and schist
with their later contortions and mineral intrusions. This is what we
see today when we examine the protruding bedrocks and the occasional stone fragments that lie on the ground.

Valleys often mark the lines of the major geologic faults that
occurred during the eons in which all this dynamic activity was taking place. Trending in a generally east–west direction, they became
the courses of streambeds and later the logical routes for crosstown
streets. At the northern end of Manhattan, the Dyckman Street

fault bisects the Fort Washington ridge of Manhattan schist, separating Fort Tryon Park and the Cloisters from Inwood Hill Park. A little farther south, 155th Street is aligned along another fault zone. The deepest and most conspicuous of the fault valleys extends from the Hudson River across 125th Street, bending diagonally south to enter the East River at 96th Street. Following Broadway from 72nd Street to Columbus Circle, another fault zone continues south to enter the East River at 23rd Street.

Burnished by Ice

It is important to emphasize that today's surface exposures of gneiss, marble, and schist are mere remnants of ranges of towering mountain peaks that were created by repeated cycles of sedimentation followed by metamorphic deformation. It was only after hundreds of millions of years that these mountain ranges were leveled by erosion and their subsurfaces exposed as the immense overburden gradually washed away. Their subsequent cracking into fault zones and the erasure of most of the sedimentary deposits from their surfaces set the stage for a new act in New York City's long and continuing geologic drama: the age of glaciation.

In all, four huge ice sheets pushed down from the north to cover portions of Europe and North America. The last and most important, whose passage is imprinted on the landscape of the modern city, was the Wisconsin advance, beginning less than a hundred thousand years ago. As the earth's climate became colder, winters lengthened and accumulated snows packed together into a frozen ice mass. At an estimated rate of a foot a day the great ice sheet moved ponderously southward. In the process the gathered fragments it contained scoured and polished exposed surfaces of bedrock. Today, glacial striations—grooves running northeast to southwest—mark its passage over the outcroppings of many rock surfaces in New York City, most noticeably those in Central Park. Finally, some 17,000 years ago, the ice stabilized, its southern edge tracing a line midway along the length of Long Island and the central spine of part of Staten Island. Manhattan and the Bronx lay deeply buried under a thousand feet of ice and frozen glacial debris.

When the winters became warmer, however, the ice sheet retreated, and its meltwaters deposited their load of sand and rocks and boulders. The southernmost edge of this unburdening, called the terminal moraine, is composed of a series of mounds marking the final stage of the glacier's advance. New York City's morainal topography constitutes the hilly parts of Staten Island, Brooklyn, and Queens. The terminal moraine at the point where the glacier halted at the mouth of the Hudson River constricted New York Bay into the Narrows, leaving an elevated bracket of defense outposts (Fort Hamilton in Brooklyn and Fort Wadsworth on Staten Island). Not only was this an ideal geographical configuration from a military perspective but it also provided for a harbor with an ample, protected shoreline for numerous docks. Thus, geology is the foundation of New York's status as one of the great port cities of the world.

The postglacial landscape of these portions of New York is what geologists call knob and kettle country, a landscape that consists of surface depressions alternating with low, rounded hills. The kettles, which were formed by melting chunks of ice that had been trapped in the moraine, can be seen as boggy wet basins of varying dimensions. These have shrunk from their original size, for as the land became once again covered by green and living things, plants encroached upon their still waters, and year by year leaves and eroded debris from the surrounding slopes have layered their depths with organic and mineral deposits, while also creating knobs adjacent to them.

Other evidence of glacial passage over the New York City landscape is found in the form of large boulders, called erratics, which can be seen in all five boroughs. The often precariously perched erratics of Central Park and the New York Botanical Garden in the Bronx are, for the most part, chunks of igneous diabase plucked by the glacier from the New Jersey Palisades or lumps of metamorphic rock yanked from the Hudson Highlands. By contrast, the erratic boulders on Long Island more frequently resemble metamorphic rocks of Connecticut origin. The unglaciated portions of the city—the southern tip of Staten Island and southern Brooklyn and Queens—became part of a vast outwash plain. Carried by coursing glacial meltwaters, deposits of sand and gravel spread out to form the flat alluvial landscape that would later remind early Dutch settlers of Holland. Postglacial movements of moraine sands from east to west along the Long Island coastline created a chain of barrier beaches. In New York City the Rockaway Peninsula, the barrier beach for Jamaica Bay, continues to push westward an estimated two hundred feet per year, or roughly one mile every twenty-five years.

Here and Now

During the past three hundred years—the last fraction of a second on the geologic clock—human beings have undoubtedly been the major environmental agents and sculptors of the New York City landscape, chopping down forests of trees to make way for a forest of buildings; dredging rivers and bays and spanning them with beautifully engineered suspension bridges; filling in marshy inlets and rechanneling streams into a network of sewers; and blasting away bedrock to create the world's largest system of underground transportation tunnels.

Still, though encrusted with pavements and buildings, the old landforms can be discerned: the gneiss and schist escarpments of the Bronx and Manhattan rearing above the flat valleys and plains of Inwood marble; the rolling morainal hills of northern Brooklyn and Queens; the flat, alluvial, glacial-outwash plain fanning out to embrace Jamaica Bay; the opening where ocean tides sever the terminal moraine, thereby creating the harbor entrance called the Narrows; and, protruding here and there from beneath its cover of glacial till, the greenish serpentine, the firm core that pushes Staten Island up out of the sea.

Tantalizing transitory glimpses of the geology of the city are offered to sidewalk superintendents by new building excavations. For more extended field exploration, there are the parks. In Pelham

Bay Park you will find the most southerly segments of the rocky coastline characteristic of New England and eastern Canada. This is a glaciated or "drowned" coast, different in appearance from the mature alluvial, unglaciated barrier-beach coastlines of Long Island and New Jersey. The origin of these Pelham Bay rocks is still something of an enigma; geology students attack them with hammers because their relationship to the rest of the New York City formations has not yet been scientifically established, making them an ideal subject for doctoral dissertations. In Central Park you can study bedrock outcroppings of mica schist ribboned with granite intrusions and grooved with glacial scratches—evidence of the northeast-to-southwest movement of the Wisconsin ice sheet. You will also find throughout the park curiously poised erratics left behind when the ice that carried them melted.

Morningside Park in Manhattan has a tall vertical wall of schist once used by mountain climbers for rock-scaling practice. Inwood Hill Park and Fort Tryon Park—twin elevations of Manhattan schist bisected by the Dyckman Street fault valley—form the northerly extension of the Fort Washington ridge, the site of Morningside Park. In Inwood Hill Park you can find glacial potholes: bowl-like depressions scoured out of the bedrock by the gravel-laden meltwaters of the glacier.

Glacial action can be seen also in the rolling terrain of Prospect Park in Brooklyn, which was modeled by the lumpy gravels of the terminal moraine. Kettlehole ponds created by melting ice trapped within it are found at High Rock Park on Staten Island, Highland Park in Brooklyn, and Alley Pond Park and Cunningham Park in Queens. A green layer of duckweed floats on their placid surfaces, and skunk cabbages and swamp maples fringe their spongy, peaty borders. Jamaica Bay and the Rockaways present more volatile scenes as coastal geology, abetted by climate change, gnaws at the city's marine landscapes.

The conclusion of this slow but inexorably mutable process is the contemporary realization that, while the geological clock is forever ticking and the slow erosion of the city's bedrock is hard to perceive, the dynamics of change are starkly evident along the city's shoreline. This is especially true today when nature, like an angry God, appears to be meting out punishment for human indifference to the welfare of the planet. While drought parches other parts of the country, devastating coastal storms like Hurricane Sandy have battered the Atlantic coastline and made New York City a vulnerable target. This brings into question our impulse to fly in the face of the predictions of climatologists, meteorologists, and oceanographers and rely instead almost entirely on technology to protect heavily populated existing shorelines. It is important to realize that nature itself is sublimely indifferent to such remedial action and that, given New York City's current geological status, its fringe of wetlands will shrink, its marshes disappear, its islands inch toward submersion, and its beaches be periodically ravaged.

This is not an excuse for inaction with regard to saving as much of the current landscape as possible. Nevertheless, the process of doing so should be one of partnership with nature rather than reliance solely on human intervention. Appreciating New York City's extraordinary geology and the forces that continue to shape its topography is a start toward a more responsible alignment of human actions with the here and now of nature's independent dynamic.

New York

A Once and Future Arcadia

(1971)

Every morning people pour out of my apartment building and file to the bus stop on the corner of East End Avenue and 79th Street. Only a few decades ago, 79th Street was a dusty road, and where the crosstown bus sits idling a little spring poured out of the ground. Just below Sloan's Supermarket where I buy groceries, another spring gushed forth. Both springs belonged to Marston's Creek, one of the many brooks and rivulets that once coursed across the East Side of Manhattan.

In fact, everywhere up and down the length of the island where today streams of people rush to meet subways and buses there were once streams of water rushing to meet the sea. There was Cedar Creek emptying into the East River at what is now 17th Street; the Saw Kill flowing through the swamp that later became the Reservoir in Central Park; Montayne's Rivulet running in an easterly direction across Harlem to its mouth at Hell Gate Bay; Sherman Creek draining the waters of the high Fort Washington ridge into the Harlem River. There were Minetta Brook flowing through Greenwich Village and many tiny rills that spilled over the rocky ledges of the Upper West Side, cascading into the Hudson. Now, invisibly, these water courses are channeled underground as sewers;

From *New York*, November 29, 1971; from *The Forests and Wetlands of New York City* (Boston: Little, Brown, 1971).

their old beds have been geometrized in conformity with the grid of streets above them. In the Bronx, Tibbetts Brook, which feeds the Van Cortlandt swamp, becomes, after draining the swamp, the Spuyten Duyvil sewer outlet. John Kieran, author of *A Natural History of New York City,* remembers when Tibbetts Brook "ran above ground through cattail marshes and wet meadows all the way from the lake outlet to the old northern loop of the Harlem River, crossing Broadway at about 240th Street en route and providing several good swimming holes to which I gave my patronage as a schoolboy."[1]

Even after they have been channeled into the city's subterranean wastewater infrastructure, some old brooks resurface as sewer outfalls. In southern Brooklyn and Queens, the tidal creeks where fresh waters used to mingle with the incoming tides are now conduits discharging the effluent from six municipal sewage treatment plants into Jamaica Bay. Though contours have been straightened and bottoms dredged, the ancient, historically evocative names, often Dutch-donated, linger on: Paerdegat Basin, Barbadoes Basin, Conch Basin, and Mott Hook.

Two early Dutch travelers, Jasper Danckaerts and Peter Sluyter, enjoyed oysters, some measuring a foot long, from what is today the anaerobic Gowanus Canal. Newtown Creek, Brooklyn's other industrial sewer, still retains at its head a now anachronistically named little promontory, Mussel Island. Besides carving channels across the face of New York, the old streams scalloped its shores, giving the waterfront a much more sinuous border than it has today. Then, instead of a regularized circumference ruled by the Army Corps of Engineers' pierhead and bulkhead lines, the shores were everywhere indented with little bays and tidal estuaries. Instead of a firm seawall there were large salt-meadow marshes that were daily bathed as the incoming tides washed over their fine mat of cordgrasses. Prominently penetrating colonial Manhattan was the Graught, a marsh inlet later covered by Broad Street. The beavers that once built their dams along its banks are memorialized today in a financial district address: Beaver Street. Memorialized too are the girls who once spread out their laundry to dry on the grassy

banks beside the pebble-bottomed little brook that later became
Maagde Paetje, or Maiden Lane.

Manhattan was not only more irregular in outline but also a good
deal narrower in those days. Like growth rings on a tree, landfill in
the form of refuse and construction debris has been deposited over
the years in encircling bands around the southern end of the island
until now Water Street is five hundred feet from the East River, and
Greenwich Street, once the waterfront thoroughfare on the west, is
equally distant from the Hudson. Where Kennedy Airport juts a concrete apron into Jamaica Bay there were once only water and a vast
tide-inundated marsh. Soundview Park in the East Bronx, Marine
Park in Brooklyn, and Great Kills Park on Staten Island are also
"reclaimed" marshlands—that is to say, phased-out garbage dumps.

The early Dutch settlers gravitated to the flat, marsh-fringed low-
lands reminiscent of the topography of Holland. In addition to New
Amsterdam in lower Manhattan, they formed villages bordering on
other New York City wetlands: Flatbush and Flatlands in Brooklyn
where the Canarsie salt meadows stretched out to embrace Jamaica
Bay; Nieu Haarlem on the *muscoota,* or marshy plain, that covered
eastern Manhattan north of 110th Street; and Nieu Dorp beside the
Great Kills marshes on Staten Island.

The American Indians were marsh people, too, weaving trails
through the cordgrasses as they went back and forth to their fishing
grounds. Archaeologists have found evidence of their occupation in
the shell heaps beside the Bartow Creek tidal inlet (obliterated by
dredging for the Olympic rowing basin in the 1950s) in Pelham Bay
Park; in the steaming kitchen middens (covered over by ball fields in
the 1930s) near Spuyten Duyvil next to the confluence of the Harlem and Hudson Rivers at the northern edge of Inwood Park; and in
the burial chambers and extensive collections of artifacts bordering
the south shore of Staten Island and the Fresh Kills marshes (now a
garbage dump).

The Indians' main trail, which led from strongholds in the
Bronx and their camp at Inwood Hill down to the little colonial
village with its wooden houses huddled against the sides of the fort,
did not skirt the shore but ran through the Manhattan forest along

the line of present-day Broadway. In the days before the Dutch had staked out their claim to lower Manhattan, the Indians had camped on the western bank of Collect Pond, a large, clear, spring-fed water body some forty feet deep where the Criminal Court Building now stands. They left a large deposit of shells, and the Dutch named the mound they had occupied Kalchhook (Shellpoint). The appelation "Collect" is thought to be a corruption of "Kalchhook" or simply a denotation of the collection of springs that irrigated the pond. The English called it Freshwater Pond and drew their water from one of its primary sources, the Teawater Spring, so named because of its reputation for being the best drinking water on the island. Carts would form long traffic-obstructing queues at the Teawater pump, which stood where Park Row and Pearl Street now intersect.

The pond was drained by two marsh-bordered streams: the eastern, called Old Wreck Brook, ran though Wolfert's Marsh into a bay now covered by the approach ramps of the Brooklyn Bridge; the western, flowing through the Lispenard Meadows, followed the line of, and later became, the canal that gave Canal Street its name. When the tide was high, the waters of the East River and the Hudson commingled in this marsh system, and Manhattan became in effect two islands instead of one.

In colonial times Collect Pond was famous for its fishing. It was so popular, in fact, that in 1734 the town fathers passed an ordinance forbidding net fishing or the catching of fish "by any other engine, machine, arts, ways or means whatsoever, other than by angling with angle rod, hook and line only."[2] The fine for ignoring this law was 20 shillings. Later the pond played a preliminary role in the history of mechanical water transportation: in 1796, eleven years before Robert Fulton's *Clermont* began commercial service on the Hudson River, the world's first steamship was given a trial run on its waters.

By this time, however, water pollution had beset New York, and Collect Pond was badly polluted and a serious health hazard. Its refuse-laden waters stank with the bodies of dead animals. The old Kalchhook on the pond's western edge had acquired an infamous reputation, first as the spot where in 1741 those accused of participating in the so-called Negro Plot were hanged and burned and later as the site of the public gallows. In 1808 it was leveled and its rubble used to fill in the pond. Streets were laid out, with present-day Centre Street running down the middle of the former pond. The miry Lispenard Meadows, where straying cattle had sometimes become trapped in the soft marsh ooze, were drained, and the tree-bordered canal was constructed.

The area where Collect Pond once stood gained an even greater notoriety in the following decades. It became a place of filthy, crowded tenements sheltering the most degraded, gin-soaked element of Victorian society. Charles Dickens, visiting America in 1842, made a point of touring the area in the company of two policemen. He wrote: "Debauchery has made the very houses prematurely old. See how the rotten beams are tumbling down, and how the patched and broken windows seem to scowl dimly, like eyes that have been hurt in drunken frays."[3]

Not only had New York begun to have serious slum-bred social ills but the physical health of all its people was being jeopardized to an ever-increasing degree by water pollution. Contamination of the Collect had foreshadowed the general degradation of the city's water sources. Yellow fever epidemics took a calamitous toll, and the sites of today's Washington Square and Madison Avenue were employed as potter's fields for the burial of plague victims. Still, the population continued to grow and was fast outstripping the remaining clean springs and wells. The year that Dickens visited America turned out to be a jubilee year for New York, for on October 14 the Croton Aqueduct was opened, carrying pure water from the mountains of northern Westchester and Putnam counties into the Central Reservoir on the site of the future Central Park. For days people celebrated the miracle, turning on new spigots with continual fascination, toasting themselves and their town with the clear, tasteless, odorless water that came out. From the mid-nineteenth century on, New York was no longer a self-contained economic unit, and its concentrated population owed its sustenance to an ever-expanding hinterland providing not only distant watersheds but also increasingly distant food sources.

The urban ills of Dickens's day, though pernicious, were highly localized, and for the most part New York was still a pleasant and salubrious place to live. "The climate," he wrote, "is somewhat of the warmest. What it would be, without the sea breezes which come from its beautiful Bay in the evening time, I will not throw myself or my readers into a fever by inquiring."[4]

Earlier journalists had also remarked on the New York climate. The Dutch patroon Adriaen van der Donck wrote, "The air in the New-Netherlands is so dry, sweet and healthy that we need not wish that it were otherwise. . . . There are no heavy damps or stinking mists in the country, and if any did arise, a northerly breeze would blow them away, and purify the air. The summer heat is not oppressive in the warmest weather, for it is mitigated by sea breezes, the northerly winds, and by showers."[5]

The fragrance of the air was noticed by Jasper Danckaerts and his traveling companion Peter Sluyter in their wanderings around New Netherland in 1679. "In passing through this island," wrote Danckaerts of Manhattan, "we saw in different gardens trees full of apples of various kinds, and so laden with peaches and other fruit that one might doubt whether there were more leaves or fruit on them."[6] Van der Donck said that peaches were so plentiful that branches frequently broke under their weight. He went on to list other fruits that the Dutch had brought with them to New Netherland: "Morecotoons (a kind of peach), apricots, several sorts of the best plums, almonds, persimmons, cornelian cherries, figs, several sorts of currants, gooseberries, calissiens, and thorn apples."[7]

Nature's own gardens were equally bountiful. According to Daniel Denton, an early resident of Jamaica, Queens, "The fruits natural to [Long] Island are Mulberries, Posimons, Grapes great and small, Huckelberries, Cramberries, Plums of several sorts, Rosberries and Strawberries, of which last is such abundance in June, that the Fields and Woods are died red: Which the Countrey-people perceiving, instantly arm themselves with bottles of Wine, Cream, and Sugar and instead of a Coat of Male, every one takes a Female upon his Horse behind him, and so rushing violently into the fields, never leave till they have disrob'd them of their red colours, and turned them into the old habit."[8]

In colonial times, tall forests covered much of the land that was to become New York City. The native trees observed by Robert Juet, who was an officer on the *Half Moon* in 1609 when Henry Hudson made his famous voyage up the river that was later named for him, were a "great store of goodly Oakes, and Walnut trees, and Chest-nut trees, ewe trees, and trees of sweet wood in great abundance."[9]

So extensive and prolific were the forests when the first settlers arrived that Van der Donck complained: "The whole country is covered with Wood, and in our manner of speaking, there is all too much of it, and in our way. Still it comes to hand to build vessels and houses, and to enclose the farms. . . . The land also is so natural to produce wood, that in a few years large trees will be grown, which I can say with certainty from my own observation; and that unless there be natural changes or great improvidence, there can be no scarcity of wood in this country."[10]

Every New Yorker is familiar with the rock outcroppings in Central Park. Once New York was studded as far south at 30th Street with surface protrusions of the tough, durable stone known as Manhattan schist. As New York's skyscrapers today impress visitors from abroad, so the rock formations themselves awed early voyagers like Danckaerts, who speaks of "ridges of very high rocks, . . . displaying themselves very majestically, and inviting all men to acknowledge in them the majesty, grandeur, power and glory of their Creator."[11]

Between two bluffs formed by rock outcroppings at the north end of Central Park was McGown's Pass where the old trunk trail of the Indians, renamed the King's Way (later the Albany Post Road or Great Post Road), ran into the wilds of upper Manhattan. Rising out of the swampy Harlem *muscoota* was Slag Berg (Snake Hill), known today as Mount Morris, with the little village of New Harlem nestled at its base. To the west, overlooking the Hudson, was a long, narrow escarpment, the Fort Washington ridge, which was then still a dense forest inhabited by Indians and wolves, and only a few intrepid Dutch farmers established boweries in the Harlem plain during the seventeenth century. The wolves were exterminated from Manhattan by the fearful settlers in 1686, and the Indians were finally forced to abandon their last ancestral stronghold on the island in 1715.

The woods were full of all sorts of fur-bearing animals, which provided a lucrative livelihood to the members of the Dutch West India Company. Describing the profitable arrangement that had been worked out, Denton said, "The Inhabitants . . . have a considerable Trade with the Indians" in furs, meat, and fish, "which they buy at an easie rate."[12] East Harlem was known by the Dutch as Otterspoor because of the many otters along its sandy stream banks. Of birds, the Dutch patroon David Pieterszoon de Vries numbered wintering geese "by the thousands" and wild turkeys ranging in weight "from thirty and thirty-six pounds to fifty pounds." Other edible fowl included partridges, meadow hens, white and gray herons, and passenger pigeons so thick in migration "that the light can hardly be discerned where they fly."[13]

The waters were as abundantly filled with fish as the skies with birds. In those days before water pollution made New York Harbor a biologically sterile sewer, Danckaerts wrote, "It is not possible to describe how this bay swarms with fish, both large and small, whales, tunnies and porpoises, whole schools of innumerable other fish, . . . which the eagles and other birds of prey swiftly seize in their talons when the fish come up to the surface."[14]

The eagles are gone now, and commercial fishing has long since been abandoned in New York Harbor. Indeed, New York seems far removed from that idyllic time when Danckaerts and his friend Sluyter "walked out a while in the pure morning air, along the margin of the clear running water of the sea, which is driven up this river at every tide."[15]

Still, there are portions of the heritage yet intact and, what is more, the promise of rapid and spontaneous recovery wherever nature is given a chance. The opportunities for reconstructing ecosystems within the city, or further obliterating them, are at hand. The realization or defeat of these opportunities lies within the realm of politics and public demand.

The Hudson River

Then and Now

(1972)

Henry James, returning east by train from his pilgrimage across the American continent in 1905, entered the Hudson Valley, which, after viewing vast uninhabited stretches of scenery, assumed to his Europeanized eyes the aspect of "a ripe old civilization." "Antique Albany" seemed to wave at him like some rosy Dutch housewife standing at a gable window. The porticoed mansions crowning the hills overlooking the river had tamed the wilderness of Natty Bumppo into a harmony of well-groomed nature and architectural elegance. The mood of the valley then was all golden and gracious, but James presciently saw that it was doomed, its scenic destruction symbolized by the very conveyance that enabled one to read its landscape "with such splendid consistency." "One must, of course," he said, "choose between dispensing with the ugly presence and enjoying the scenery by the aid of the same."[1]

To regard the river from the windows of a plane or automobile today puts you in a similarly incongruous position. Air and water pollution, together with scenic destruction from industrial plants and power-generating facilities flanking the river, have all but reversed the Jamesian view, and now it is one that is altogether unlike the landscape that greeted the other Henry, for whom the river is named, when he began his exploratory trip upstream to Albany in

From *New York*, May 29, 1972.

1609. Where majestic hemlocks then stood, now a forest of Con Ed smokestacks is growing. "The Mountaynes [that] looked as if some Metall or Minerall were in them" to Hudson's eyes have been gouged, gutted, and turned into rock quarries. The Dutch farms that sprang up along the water's edge soon after Hudson transmitted the news of the valley's fertility, its luxuriance of "Tobacco and Indian Wheat . . . Beanes . . . Grapes and Pompions," have been replaced by farms of oil-storage tanks.[2] Nevertheless, in somewhat abridged and fragmented form you can still read the legend of the river. Though the pages of its history are torn and soiled and its ecology mutilated, it is yet a fascinating document. Certainly there are enough relics of river life still in existence to keep the devoted history buff and ardent naturalist occupied for several weekends.

•

Many of the Dutch-donated place names along the river—Catskill and Peekskill, Cortlandt and Rensselaer—recall the period of the patroons, merchants who obtained vast grants of riverfront land on the condition they would colonize them with fifty or more persons. After 1664, when the lucrative Hudson corridor fell into English hands, a freehold manorial system was instituted. An enterprising businessman could, after obtaining a license to purchase from the governor, assemble sufficient lands to apply for a Royal Patent.

Frederick Philipse, a shrewd and enterprising Dutch carpenter in New York, bought Adriaen van der Donck's old patroonship in what is now the Bronx. Philipse had branched out from carpentry into shipping, and, as his wealth increased, he extended his real estate acquisitions parcel by parcel until his landholdings stretched all the way from Spuyten Duyvil to the Croton River. His mill and attendant office and barns where the Pocantico River spills into the Hudson at Tarrytown have been reconstructed as part of Sleepy Hollow restorations, the Rockefeller family's contribution to Hudson River Valley conservation. There you can see flax grown, then spun, and, when combined with wool, woven into linsey-woolsey. A ruddy-faced miller will activate the powerful waterwheel to set the millstones turning, and you can watch corn being transformed into meal.

The growing commercial prosperity of the colonial Hudson, however, was checked as the river became the central stage for the drama of the American Revolution. Strategically, possession of the river was the primary objective of both sides. If the British could hold it they would effectively sever overland communications between New England and the other Atlantic seaboard colonies. As an axis along which he could send troops either north or south, the river was absolutely crucial to Washington. It was not accidental that he set up his wartime headquarters in Newburgh. The old stone house from which he issued orders deploying patriot forces back and forth across the Hudson is now a designated historic site, as is the clapboard tavern where General Anthony Wayne had his headquarters.

The century following the Revolution marked the river's golden interlude; no longer scourged by war, not yet invaded by industry, it presented a serenely smiling face that was both bucolic and romantic. In the first three decades after the war, the sloop was the symbol of the Hudson's prosperity as well as her chief means of transportation. Before the steamboat telescoped the speed of travel from several days to several hours, a journey by river on one of these single-masted sailboats was both a momentous and an idyllic experience. Friends and well-wishers would crowd the dock before a departure; there would be tearful farewells, laying in of stores of food; then, hoping for good weather and a steady breeze, the crew would hoist sail and the voyage begin. In this period, for the first time, travelers on the Hudson began to assess their surroundings not simply in economic terms, as had the seventeenth-century explorers and eighteenth-century visitors and settlers. The river valley began to be appreciated as something else— scenery. Educated travelers of the early nineteenth century classified landscapes as "beautiful," "sublime," and "picturesque." The Hudson provided all three categories.

In 1807 the British traveler John Lambert wrote, "This river affords some of the noblest landscapes and scenery that are to be found in any part of North America. Nature and art have both contributed to render its shores at once sublime and beautiful."[3] And that same year a new era in the history of world transportation had dawned: the steamboat was born on the waters of the Hudson.

Robert Fulton's smoke-belching *Clermont* must have created a spectacle almost as astonishing as Henry Hudson's white-winged *Half Moon* two hundred years earlier. Sloops continued to tack back and forth with the Hudson's breezes, but the speed, reliability, and luxury of the "floating palaces" quickly made them the preferred mode of travel for the well-to-do.

While steamboats stimulated commerce, they also provided an opportunity for more and more people to respond romantically to nature on the Hudson. Its scenery unscrolled before such passengers as the actress Fanny Kemble, who "remained on deck without my bonnet, walking to and fro, and enjoying the delicious wind that was as bracing as a showerbath."[4]

Unlike James Fenimore Cooper, who went to the backwoods for his peculiarly American consciousness-raising themes, Washington Irving, the Hudson River Valley's first man of letters, was urbane in temperament. Echoes of Irving still emanate from the Catskills, which he peopled with comic Dutch characters and hobgoblins, and from Tarrytown, his legendary Sleepy Hollow and the site of Sunnyside, his beloved home. Sunnyside was originally intended as his vacation retreat, a romantic conceit, "a little old-fashioned stone mansion, all made up of gable ends, and as full of angles and corners as an old cocked hat."[5] He bought it from a Dutch farmer named Wolfert Ecker in 1835 and remodeled it, incorporating such novel conveniences as hot and cold running water and whimsically embellishing it with a weathervane-studded, crow-stepped roof. He called it Wolfert's Roost and turned it into a veritable henhouse of female relatives.

On my personal pilgrimage to historic sites along the Hudson, I visited Sunnyside with the expectation of finding it somewhat cutesy, a little antiseptic kernel of the past, all polished up, trim and spruce and neat. Well, yes, there were hostesses in full-blown crinolines and swans in the pond, but I soon found myself, almost against my will, falling into the ingratiating mood of the place.

Besides Irving, other writers of the Romantic era identified themselves with the Hudson River Valley wilderness, none more closely than the poet-editor William Cullen Bryant. Chauvinistically, he asserted—at a time when New Yorkers traveled abroad to admire scenery—that the western shore of the Hudson was "as worthy of a pilgrimage across the Atlantic as the Alps themselves."[6]

It was perhaps the painters even more than the writers, however, who fixed the Hudson River scenery most vividly in the American imagination. Bryant's "kindred spirit," Thomas Cole, started the movement to the mountains in 1825. Though not open to the public, Cole's Federal-style house in the town of Catskill still stands.[7] Across the Rip Van Winkle Bridge, almost directly opposite it, is Olana, the splendid, exotic, pseudo-Moorish fantasy castle of Cole's only pupil, Frederic Edwin Church. That Church, the son of a wealthy Hartford insurance man, had the means to travel widely is reflected both in the decor of Olana and in the dramatic far-away subjects he chose to paint. His sensational, reputation-establishing canvas was *Heart of the Andes;* but as John K. Howat of the Metropolitan Museum points out in his book on the Hudson River School, Church's real excellence as an artist can best be appreciated in "the fluently executed oil sketches on paper and canvas" of the scenery of the Hudson, which are scattered throughout the beautiful copper-and-russet-toned rooms of Olana.[8]

In 1860, the year following the exhibition of *Heart of the Andes,* Jasper Cropsey, another second-generation artist of the Hudson River School, decided to emulate Church's success with an ambitiously scaled painting of a North American landscape subject. The result was *Autumn – On the Hudson River,* now in the National Gallery in Washington. The zenith of his career occurred in 1865, and the optimism born of a $3,500 sale he made of one painting that year prompted him to build his dream castle retreat-cum-studio, Aladdin, in Warwick, New York. But, like Church and other artists of the Hudson River School, Cropsey's reputation went quickly downhill during the 1870s as landscape painting went out of vogue, and, lacking Church's independent income, he was forced to abandon Aladdin and move to Hastings-on-Hudson. Even in reduced circumstances he lived comfortably—almost elegantly—in a delightful Victorian Gothic "cottage" overlooking the river.

The river's golden age, the age of Irving and Cropsey, gave way to the Gilded Age. To understand the difference between gold and gilt and gain a glimpse of vulgarity triumphant, visit the Vanderbilt estate in Hyde Park. The site is historic, once owned by Dr. John Bard and later by his son, Samuel Bard, physician to George Washington. After Samuel Bard's death it was acquired by his fellow physician Dr. David Hosack, who was an avid botanist. Hosack spent large sums of money landscaping the estate with rare imported specimen trees, and the place was a famous showpiece in his day. Five years after Hosack died in 1835, John Jacob Astor acquired the property, and his heirs, the Walter Langdons, lived there until 1894, when Frederick W. Vanderbilt purchased it and hired McKim, Mead & White to build a neo–Italian Renaissance mansion of mind-boggling opulence. No European palace-aping bit of aristocratic status decor is missing: the Carrara marble busts, the hand-carved wood paneling (done by Swiss artisans specially imported for the task), the banal genre scene paintings, presumably souvenirs of travels abroad. The velvets and damasks and marble and plaster are concocted into such a rich and overwrought vanity confection of cream and green and pink and gold that it all becomes a bit nauseating.

The Vanderbilt glut of grandeur comes toward the end of a long series of architectural embellishments, a large and gaudy rhinestone set in the Hudson's necklace of villas and stately homes. Throughout the nineteenth century there was much debate about the comparative beauties of American and European scenery. Many times over the Hudson was called the American Rhine. Some chauvinists maintained that its unadorned beauty surpassed that of the romantically castled European river; in opposition other native Romanticists held that something approaching the mellow antique effects of the castles on the Rhine was necessary to give the Hudson a truly picturesque appearance. It was the old argument, so pervasive in nineteenth-century American debate, of wilderness versus civilization. Cole and his followers voted for the wilderness aesthetic. Indeed, the national self-image that found articulation in Emerson's famous 1836 essay "Nature" made God and nature indissoluble. But the "Bitch Goddess" of Materialism, of Civilization and Success, had already entered the race, and after the Civil War she would nose ahead to finish a hands-down winner.

Of course, the whole story of the river isn't told by the travelers or the artists or the pre-income-tax rich. There were, and to some extent still are, the rivermen—ferrymen, bargemen, tugmen, steamboat captains—people for whom the river has traditionally represented a livelihood and a way of life. The river's importance economically is a result of its ecology, which in turn is a result of the forces of geology and climate.

According to the geologist Christopher Schuberth of the American Museum of Natural History, the lower Hudson was not always as straight as it is now. There is evidence that just north of the tall colonnaded cliff of the Palisades at Sparkill its course meandered off to the west, cutting a series of water gaps (present-day wind gaps) through the ridges of New Jersey until it veered eastward to empty into Raritan Bay. Eventually, however, erosion caused a smaller stream paralleling the Palisades on the east to extend its headwaters northward until, about ten or fifteen million years ago, it captured the Hudson at Sparkill.

In addition to the visible river, there is a wide and very deep channel extending 150 miles out onto the continental shelf. This channel is a legacy of the time when glacial ice covered North America and the seas diminished as some of their waters were sucked into the great frozen shield, their retreating margins leaving a broad alluvial coastal plain. As the earth warmed up, the ancient Hudson, which had been a river for millions of years already, flushed out the meltwaters of the ice sheet across the sandy plain, thus carving the now invisible canyon. The replenished seas, which drowned the lower half of the old river valley and submerged the canyon, then began sending tidal currents like springtime sap flowing upstream. The Hudson south of present-day Troy is therefore not a river at all but rather an estuary where the waters of mountain streams mingle with those of the Atlantic.

•

It is the nature of estuaries to be extremely fertile ecosystems, and the Hudson has been particularly bountiful and prolific. Its shores were, and in some places, like Constitution Island and Piermont, still are, fringed with *Spartina,* the nutritious salt-marsh grass that disintegrates into detritus to provide food for zooplankton and benthic (mud-bottom) organisms. In addition to having been a good feeding ground, the Hudson has served as an excellent breeding place, its protected marsh coves and gently oscillating tidal waters acting as incubators for the eggs laid on the spring spawning runs of sea sturgeon, shad, and striped bass. Estuaries are also the natural nurseries of shellfish. Bedloe's (now Liberty) Island at the mouth of the Hudson was once called Oyster Island, and oyster beds extended all the way up to Ossining. The Dutch and English were mollusk-lovers and ate quantities of Hudson River oysters and crushed their shells for gravel, lime, and even wig powder.

The Swedish naturalist Peter Kalm, who had come to America to catalog New World flora for the great botanist Linnaeus, wrote in 1749: "Some porpoises played and tumbled in the river. . . . Every now and then we saw several kinds of fish leaping out of the water. . . . The porpoises seldom go higher up the Hudson River than the salt water goes; after that, the sturgeons fill their place. It has however sometimes happened that porpoises have gone clear up to Albany. . . . There is a report that a whale once came up river to this town."[9]

Today, dredging has destroyed all but a vestige of the beds of Hudson River oysters, and frolicking porpoises are a sight of the past. Bridges of suspended steel have replaced ferries, and now the only sloop that plies the Hudson's once sail-flecked waters is the *Clearwater,* tacking from shore to shore with her message of river revival and regeneration delivered to the tune of Pete Seeger's banjo. The last of the side-wheelers, the Day Line's *Alexander Hamilton,* has forever ceased to churn the river's waters, and refrigeration and water pollution have made its once profitable ice-cutting industry obsolete.

The death of a river is not a pretty sight. The awesome wilderness that so engaged the imaginations of nineteenth-century writers and painters, making the scenery of the Hudson the very metaphor for the American wilderness until after the Civil War, is now scored and scarred by highways, its trackless forests incised by railroad tracks, its sleepy hollows filled with housing developments. The inlet where Frederick Philipse's sloops once wended their way into the mouth of the Pocantico Hills is now obstructed by a General Motors assembly plant. There is only one vast modern-day patroon-ship, Pocantico Hills (the Rockefeller family estate), 3,500 acres of manicured meadows and forested ridges stretching from Route 9 to the Saw Mill River Parkway. The Gilded Age is gone, and the castles and manor houses have been turned over to tourists or converted into schools. Certainly, Fanny Kemble would no longer be able to enjoy "the delicious wind" if she were to cruise too near one of the many sewer outfalls that empty into the river.

To measure the loss, our loss, listen to Washington Irving:

What a time of intense delight was that first sail through the Highlands! I sat on the deck as we slowly tided along at the foot of those stern mountains, and gazed with wonder and admiration at cliffs impending far above me, crowned with forests, with eagles sailing and screaming around them; or listened to the unseen stream dashing down precipices; or beheld rock, and tree, and cloud, and sky reflected in the glassy stream of the river. And then how solemn and thrilling the scene as we anchored at night at the foot of these mountains, clothed with overhanging forests; and everything grew dark and mysterious; and I heard the plaintive note of the whip-poor-will from the mountain-side, or was startled now and then by the sudden leap and heavy splash of the sturgeon.[10]

Yet it would be premature to write the obituary of the Hudson. The river itself still lives, its powerful current alternating direction with the tides.

"An American Kew"

The Transformation of Bronx Park into the New York Botanical Garden

(2014)

The New York Botanical Garden's origins can be traced to three important aspects of nineteenth-century American culture: reform humanitarianism, the beginning of scientific botany as a professional occupation, and Gilded Age civic pride. This is the story of how these forces and the women and men who embodied them resulted in a landscape that is a notable pleasure ground, a showcase of various plant collections, and home to several structures of architectural grandeur, research utility, and educational purpose.

No landscape and no institution remains in stasis, and although much of the nineteenth-century heritage of the Garden is a living legacy, subsequent layers of societal values and design intentions have inscribed its 250 acres with newer elements, a process that continues in the twenty-first century. My purpose here will be to investigate this palimpsest as a dynamic cultural landscape, changing over time through both innovation and preservation. In doing so, we must necessarily take into consideration the aesthetic tenets of nineteenth-century landscape architecture and the inherent problem of combining the prevailing taste for the picturesque style, with its affinity for naturalistic composition, and the desire to foster

A shorter version of this essay appeared in *Flora Illustrata: Great Works from the LuEsther T. Mertz Library of The New York Botanical Garden,* ed. Susan M. Fraser and Vanessa Bezemer Sellers (New York: The New York Botanical Garden; New Haven: Yale University Press, 2014).

botanical education by arranging plants in unitary groupings of like species. Added to this challenge was the integration of neoclassical buildings of monumental proportions within a Victorian pleasure ground where, by contrast, architecture is typically small in scale and primarily intended to ornament certain points within the landscape rather than serve as major features.

.

To understand how the design and building of the New York Botanical Garden played out within this period of transforming taste, it is useful to consider New York City's nineteenth-century parks movement. Surmounting the fears of some prejudiced opponents who felt the immigrant "hoi polloi" would abuse a public space that welcomed both the wealthy and the poor, certain visionary citizens who foresaw the city's future as a great commercial metropolis spurred the successful political campaign that resulted in the 1853 legislation exempting the acreage set aside for the park from the confines of Manhattan's grid plat. Through their civic activism Central Park came into being. But the mere reservation of land by withholding it from development was only a prerequisite; the park had to be designed, managed, and made safe and accessible throughout if it were to fulfill its purpose as a public amenity. The question was in what manner this should be undertaken.

"Greensward," the name Frederic Law Olmsted and Calvert Vaux gave to their winning entry in the 1858 design competition for Central Park, is a triumph of nineteenth-century engineering infrastructure overlaid by a naturalistic landscape designed according to aesthetic principles harking back to eighteenth-century England. Allied with the Romantic movement, this style continued to direct park design throughout much of the nineteenth century in spite of the fact that a newer style, the gardenesque, promulgated by John Claudius Loudon in England, was in vogue at the time that Olmsted and Vaux designed Central Park. In contrast to Loudon, Olmsted and Vaux were firm in their belief that a *rus in urbe*—an illusion of open countryside within the confines of the city—was a superior design motive to one whose chief aim was botanical display and education.

In its favor, the gardenesque was a landscape design idiom well suited to the period in which new plant species from around the world were being collected and naturalized in Western gardens. Moreover, since Andrew Jackson Downing, who was a nurseryman as well as an admirer of Loudon, had been a vigorous champion of the creation of a great park for New York City and, as America's foremost landscape-design authority, the logical candidate to design it, one may speculate as to the form its plan might have taken had he not met an untimely death a year before the legislation creating the park was passed. Judging by the essays he wrote for *The Horticulturist,* the magazine he edited, it would have probably blended the gardenesque with the picturesque to a much greater extent than was the case with the Olmsted-Vaux Greensward plan.

When Downing visited England in 1850, he had made a point of seeing the Derby Arboretum, recently designed by Loudon, as well as the Royal Botanic Garden at Kew where he spent an entire day with Sir William Hooker, the eminent botanist who was its first director. He had nothing but the highest praise for the way the 200-acre site was divided into a pleasure ground of 140 acres and a 60-acre botanic garden proper.[1] Further, he was ecstatic in his description of Kew's enormous, recently built palm house: "It is a palace of glass—362 feet in length, and 66 feet high—and fairy-like and elegant in its proportions, though of great strength; for the whole, framework and sashes, is of cast iron, glazed with 45,000 feet of glass. . . . From the light iron gallery, . . . you look down on the richest assemblage of vegetable forms that can be conceived; while over your head clamber, under the iron rafters, in charming luxuriance, the richest passion flowers and other vines of the East Indian Islands." What struck him most forcibly was the fact that the gardens at Kew were thronged with "a thousand or twelve hundred men, women and children of all ages, —well dressed, orderly and neat, and examining all with interest and delight."[2]

The following year, with these impressions still fresh in his mind, Downing set forth an imaginative vision for a great park of five hundred or more acres for New York City, in which would be built "winter gardens of glass, like the great Crystal Palace, where the whole people could luxuriate in groves of the palms and spice trees of the tropics, at the same moment that sleighing parties glided swiftly and noiselessly over the snow-covered surface of the country-like avenues of the wintry park without."[3]

The pressure on Central Park to be a receptacle for all sorts of monumental civic architecture, memorials, and sports facilities would continue throughout much of its history, and it did become the site for a number of these things, including most conspicuously the Metropolitan Museum. Fortunately, however, it was not for long the only option for siting such projects. The pioneering achievement of creating this purpose-built people's park, which served as a model and stimulus for other cities to build large public parks, also sparked a movement to create additional parks in New York City itself. In 1881 a second generation of foresighted citizens formed the New York Park Association in order to lobby for the creation of an entire system of parkway-linked parks north of the Harlem River.

The association's prime mover was a newspaper reporter and editor, John Mullaly. After three years of contentious wrangling between advocates and opponents, in 1884 Mullaly and his cohorts were successful in their campaign for the enactment by the New York State Legislature of a bill that set aside 3,840 acres of land in the still undeveloped region between Long Island Sound and the Hudson River, now the Bronx, for six new parks—Pelham Bay, Van Cortlandt, Bronx, St. Mary's, Claremont, and Crotona—and three parkways—Mosholu, Bronx, and Pelham. In 1887, in the wake of this political achievement, Mullaly penned a narrative titled *The New Parks beyond the Harlem* in which he described with florid fervor the scenic attributes and practical advantages of their individual sites.

According to him, no extraordinary feat of engineering and design, as in the case of Central Park, would be necessary, so well endowed by nature were they already. At the same time, he envisioned a host of recreational uses that they could accommodate: "a Parade Ground, a Rifle Range, Base Ball, Lacrosse, Polo, Tennis and all athletic games; picnic and excursion parties, and nine mile of waterfront for bathing, fishing, yachting and rowing."[4] And when it came to "rare sylvan beauties," Mullaly held that no other park was more lovely than Bronx Park, "for the character of the scenery is so varied that every step is a surprise and the artist and 'the wayfaring man might love to linger there.' . . . The banks [of the Bronx River] rise to the height of fifty, eighty and even ninety feet; in some places abrupt and precipitous, in others easily surmounted. Gigantic trees, centuries old, crown these summits, while great moss and ivy-covered rocks project here and there at different heights above the surface of the river, increasing the wildness of the scene."[5] With its magnificent tree known as "De Lancey's ancient pine," a conspicuously large glacial erratic balancing on a rock ledge, and its scenic river glade, Bronx Park was already a favorite haunt of prominent artists of the day.

But Bronx Park was envisioned by Mullaly as more than an artists' haunt. "No better place could be selected for a model botanical garden than Bronx Park," he declared, "and no better use could be made of any of the parks than to make them subserve educational purposes, practical schools of horticulture, zoology, arboriculture, etc., where children could learn without studying, acquire knowledge without opening a book, and where there could be levied 'a tax of profit from their very play.'" Expatiating on this theme, he wrote, "Such an institution would teach the true value of trees, show that they had a higher mission to fulfill than beautifying the landscape or affording grateful shade to the exhausted traveler; that they added to the fertility of our soil and increased the flow of our rivers, and thus made commerce and agriculture their debtors." In short, Mullaly argued, "A grand botanical garden in the Bronx Park would be the right thing in the right place."[6]

•

The achievement of Mullaly's dream would necessitate yet another campaign by private citizens, and to turn it into reality would require those who were able to make a clear and persuasive case for the need to provide an institution dedicated to the advance of the science of botany as well as to the display of plants. It would also need funding. Happily in this regard, by the end of the nineteenth century New York was home to some of the country's wealthiest post–Civil War industrial and financial magnates, and their philanthropic support of the Garden's beginnings was immediately forthcoming. But civic ambition and money were only part of the equation. A clear vision and the leadership and management skills to realize such an immense project, embracing the building of both an institutional structure and the landscape and buildings that gave it substance, were necessary as well. Fortunately, such a visionary leader was at hand.

Both as an institution and as a landscape, much of the New York Botanical Garden as we know it today represents the life work of Nathaniel Lord Britton, its first director, who oversaw the Garden's creation and construction from its inception in 1895 until 1929. His wife, Elizabeth Knight Britton, a bryologist (student of liverworts and mosses) and Britton's lifelong collaborator in botanical research, was of invaluable assistance in this endeavor. Both Brittons were members of the Torrey Botanical Club (later called the Torrey Botanical Society), which was started in the 1860s by the botanist John Torrey, and they carried back from their wedding trip in England an overwhelming impression of the Royal Botanic Garden at Kew.

Just as the parks of England had served as a competitive stimulus for the creation of Central Park, so now the notion of "an American Kew," as the *New York Herald* dubbed it, took shape in the popular imagination.[7] Following Mrs. Britton's description of Kew at a Torrey Club meeting in October 1888, a committee of the club formed and on January 8, 1889, resolved to appeal to the Department of Public Parks "for adequate space in one of the city parks, if any individual or organization should provide sufficient means for the establishment of [a botanical] garden." At a meeting a few months later in the home of Mrs. Charles P. Daly, "it was resolved to ask the necessary permission from the Legislature of the State of New York to enable the Department of Parks to appropriate land for a site in Bronx Park for the proposed garden, . . . [and] there was some discussion as regards the most favorable and desirable site, but the northern end of Bronx Park was agreed upon as the best."[8]

In 1891 the state legislature's Act of Incorporation creating the New York Botanical Garden, which contained the requirement that $250,000 be raised from the private sector, was approved by the governor.[9] Bylaws were drawn up, and a finance committee and an auxiliary committee made up of fourteen women were formed. The corporation was to be overseen by a board of managers consisting of the president of Columbia College and its professors of botany, geology, and chemistry, the president of the Torrey Botanical Club, the president of the New York City Board of Education, the mayor, and the president of the Board of Commissioners of the Department of Public Parks, along with nine elected members.

By 1895 the necessary subscriptions totaling $250,000 had been raised from twenty-one wealthy men, with major contributions by Andrew Carnegie, J. P. Morgan, John D. Rockefeller, and Cornelius Vanderbilt II, along with Columbia College, which considered the Garden from its inception as an allied institution for botanical research. The newly formed board appointed Nathaniel Lord Britton as secretary of the board and director-in-chief of the Garden.

The question remained as to the selection of the exact boundaries of the Garden's 250 acres within the 653-acre Bronx Park. Being a private institution sited on public property meant that the board of the Garden needed to obtain the city's permission in this matter, and in any case the members were intent upon seeking the best advice possible. As New York's foremost landscape designers and consultants to the Department of Public Parks, Calvert Vaux— Olmsted's former partner—and the landscape architect Samuel Parsons Jr. were the logical authorities to reconnoiter the site with Britton and two other members of the subcommittee formed for the purpose of planning the Garden's layout. The boundaries they chose encompassed much of the former estates of the Lorillard family lying in the northern part of the park. A native hemlock forest, a picturesque old snuff mill, and a beautiful portion of the Bronx River where it meandered through a hill-bordered valley and several massive rock outcrops were among the scenic assets. The result of this consensus was a map signed by Vaux and Parsons showing the proposed Garden boundaries, existing buildings, and abutting and interior roads. With the official approval of a resolution by the Board of Parks, the land was transferred to management of the trustees and president of the Garden.

In moving forward with the layout of the Garden, the board thought it desirable to obtain the advice of a recognized landscape professional, and according to the minutes of a meeting held on December 6, 1895, in the office of Cornelius Vanderbilt, "the subcommittee was given authority to consult Mr. F. L. Olmsted or other landscape engineers." Olmsted, who lived in Boston, was by this time in poor health, and Vaux had recently died. The board therefore turned to John Rowlett Brinley, a civil and landscape engineer who had formerly worked on a surveying project with Olmsted's sons, the inheritors of their father's practice. As it turned out, Brinley would remain the Garden's primary landscape consultant for the next thirty-six years.[10]

Both the Vaux-Parsons topographical survey and a 1900 schematic map signed by Brinley constitute key documents recording the formation of the Garden's landscape. In each of these the Hemlock Grove is marked out as remnant native forest and deemed a sacrosanct portion of the design, an area to be left in its natural state. The Brinley map depicts several features of the site as subsequently realized, including the museum crowning the hill near the main entrance next to the train station. Grand and symmetrical in outline, it was intended to be, along with a magnificent conservatory, the Garden's most important building. Also specified were discrete sections for individual collections of deciduous trees, shrubs, and herbs as well as a marshy section considered suitable for a five-acre bog garden for aquatic plants. Another low-lying wetland north of the museum site was planned for the creation of two adjacent lakes.

•

To read the minutes of the newly formed board of the New York Botanical Garden, which was initially chaired by Cornelius Vanderbilt, in the archive of the Garden's LuEsther T. Mertz Library is to watch the Garden take shape before one's eyes. All of these typescript minutes were signed, as were subsequent ones during his long tenure as director-in-chief, by N. L. Britton, Secretary. Clearly, the hand that wielded the pen was the same hand that continued to guide the Garden as it was being transformed into an important scientific institution and pleasure ground during the early years of the twentieth century. The building of the institution's board went hand in hand with Britton's building of the Garden's campus. Thus the minutes of January 13, 1913, record the election of J. Pierpont Morgan, Henry Clay Frick, and other philanthropic magnates as trustees, and the following November these gentlemen were joined by several other members of New York's social elite, a group that included Jacob Schiff, Louis Comfort Tiffany, John Auchincloss, William K. Vanderbilt, William Vincent Astor, and Ogden Mills. At the same meeting, three women and six men were nominated to fill vacancies on the board, and twelve women were recommended for election as auxiliary members of the legally chartered nonprofit corporation responsible for the Garden's finances, management, landscape design, and further botanical development.

In addition to recording the various stages of the Garden as it was being built, the minutes also contain information about the important acquisitions that the Garden accrued as time went on. Torrey, who had been named an emeritus professor of chemistry and botany and a trustee of Columbia College, had donated his herbarium of 50,000 specimens to that institution. During his tenure as Columbia's president between 1890 and 1901, Seth Low, a strong advocate of the Garden as an essential component of botanical studies, oversaw the transfer of Torrey's herbarium, along with a collection of Characeae (fossil plants from Carboniferous-period coal deposits) and other plants from the University Botanical Museum to the Garden. In addition, Columbia's collection of paleobotanical books was placed in the library of the new museum after it was constructed. On April 26, 1912, the board voted its approval of Britton's acquisition of a collection of Darwiniana for $5,000. Such holdings became the core of what are now the Mertz Library's collections.

Working on several fronts from the beginning, Britton inaugurated a series of public lectures, started the publication of a bulletin and a journal, initiated a graduate program for Columbia students, and fielded scientific research stations in Puerto Rico and Jamaica. Along with this institutional mission development, improvement of the grounds and construction of the museum, conservatory, and greenhouses and other horticultural facilities necessary for botanical education and display proceeded apace according to the official plan prepared in 1896 by Brinley in conjunction with Parsons and several other figures: Samuel Henshaw, head gardener; Lucien Underwood, a professor on the Board of Scientific Directors at Columbia College; architect Robert W. Gibson; and Lincoln Pierson, a representative of the Lord & Burnham firm.[11]

As was true for the building of Central Park, a hydrological infrastructure was necessary, as was good drainage, which in this case could be assisted by lowering the dam beside the snuff mill. Also, again as in Central Park, circulation was an underlying necessity in providing a pleasurable experience for visitors as they moved from one type of Garden scenery to another. Constructing the circuit of drives of crushed stone and gravel along the route originally proposed by Calvert Vaux and Samuel Parsons progressed year by year. At the same time, paths were laid and several thousand linear feet of 16-inch-high iron guardrails were installed alongside to protect the new plantings. Like Central Park, glacier-scoured Bronx Park had only a thin soil cover, and therefore topsoil had to be imported in great quantities both to ensure an adequate depth for tree roots and to permit grading the ground's surface to form a series of gentle swells.

By 1900 head gardener George Nash and the laborers working under him had established eight separate plantations in the Garden. In accordance with the 1896 plan, these were arranged according to types of plant collections: the herbaceous beds, a fruticetum for shrubs, a salicetum for the cultivation of willows and poplars, a pinetum for coniferous evergreens, and a viticetum for vines. A boundary screen served as a supplemental nursery and display border. Although somewhat at odds with the rest of the naturalistic landscape, an axial allée of tulip trees in keeping with the neoclassical symmetry of the museum was planted in front of its main entrance in 1903. Other plantings, such as an eight-acre teaching garden with taxonomic labels, intended to instruct viewers in the principles of botanical systematization, were integrated into the parklike grounds.

These attempts to graft onto the sylvan scenery extolled by Mullaly both the educational features of a world-class botanical garden and the grandeur of Gilded Age neoclassical architecture encapsulate the underlying difficulty of maintaining a coherent aesthetic throughout the entire site. But due respect was paid to Romantic design principles in the Hemlock Grove and the wooded gorge next to it, which were managed as remnants of the original Bronx Park landscape with its native vegetation of beech, chestnut, sweet birch, red maple, hickory, oaks, dogwood, and tulip trees mixed with the hemlocks. Natural, rather than paved, paths and log railings instead of iron ones helped preserve the rustic appearance of this area of the Garden.

Ground was broken for Robert W. Gibson's imposing museum in 1898, but the grandest element in the Garden's landscape—at once both educational and monumental—was the Lord & Burnham conservatory, a cynosure that, much to the satisfaction of the Garden's founders, did in fact rival the great Palm House at Kew. Its construction began in 1899 on a site that was not aligned with the museum as intended in the original plan but was still situated so that its huge dome, the Garden's icon to this day, was clearly visible from the main entrance. In the early years of the twentieth century, a boundary fence with iron pickets and stone piers designed by Brinley began to be built in sections. Brinley also designed a handsome Italianate stone bridge to carry the newly built drive over the Twin Lakes, which had been constructed in 1901 by damming a Bronx River tributary stream and capturing adjacent watershed drainage.

In 1915 the existing site constraints and the Garden's desire to display more plant collections within broad lawns led Britton and the board's president, W. Gilman Thompson, to put forth a request to the city for the annexation of adjacent land. The transfer of property, which included the Lorillard mansion, a lake, and existing greenhouses, was granted with the caveat that the parks department could reserve some grounds for public picnicking as well as certain facilities for its own use. The addition of this 140-acre parcel brought the Garden's size to a total of approximately 400 acres. After some clearing, grading, and the extension of drives, paths, and infrastructure into this area, it was possible to create a new entrance and a rock garden. The acquisition of the additional land also made it possible for the board to commission the landscape designer Beatrix Jones Farrand to create a triangular-shaped rose garden in a one-and-a-half-acre dell.[12]

Reading the correspondence between Britton and Farrand in the Mertz Library gives an immediacy to the design process as it progressed from its inception, beginning with Farrand's July 20, 1915, telegram from her summer home in Maine, saying, "Invitation to cooperate with Mr. Brinley in planning new rose garden just received—eager to help in that particular work." In a letter of October 7 she writes: "Thank you very much for the photographs, which are precisely what I want. The 'inward eye' of the camera has given me just the views that will help, and when Mr. Brinley's survey comes, I can start more definitely on the plan of the ground." On October 20 she asserts that enclosure of the rose garden is essential in order "to prevent possible theft of what will undoubtedly be a display calculated to arouse the envy of rosarians. . . . Enclosure will, of course, be ornamental and would be a very attractive way of displaying all the climbing roses." On November 18, after exploring various schemes and settling on the general outlines of her preliminary design, she declared, "The lines of the valley are not to be contradicted, and the plan must be made to fit the ground rather than an attempt made to ignore the natural conditions and impose a regular design." In the notes appended to her letter, she explains the way in which the beds were to be arranged:

> The central arbor is designed to show the stronger growing sorts of climbing roses. . . . The beds around it are designed for a display of the smaller so-called ever-blooming roses of the Hermosa or Perle d'Or types, and on the outer circle of these beds a collection of the smaller growing climbing roses,

grown on iron standards and chains, as shown on the plan, would give a background to the lower growing kinds and a setting to the summer house. Certain divisions of the rectangular beds may be used to grow roses of a type such as hybrid teas or hybrid perpetuals, thus keeping these classes together. The outer border is designed for the larger growing horticultural varieties of bush roses, such as the hybrid rugosas, sweet briars, Scotch roses, etc.

The final result was a plan in which turf paths separated 139 polygonal beds of different sizes arranged concentrically around a central arbor.

Obtaining board approval for Farrand's plan of the Rose Garden was one thing; underwriting its cost was another. Britton solicited the members of the corporation and the women's auxiliary committee for contributions, and Farrand was quick to add her own fundraising suggestion. "What do you think of getting estimates in separate sections, so that they could be tabulated and dangled before prospective subscribers?" she wrote Britton. Nudged by his wife, George W. Perkins became an early subscriber to the Rose Garden fund, and more wealthy New Yorkers followed suit.

Britton obviously saw how this approach to raising money could aid his ambitious program of adorning other parts of the Garden with handsome gates, bridges, fountains, and garden shelters. Assisted by Louis F. Bird, a talented watercolorist, Brinley prepared a set of watercolor paintings representing the as yet unbuilt structures in the Garden. These beautiful renderings, which can now be viewed in the Mertz Library, are accompanied by marginal annotations in pencil of the cost of various features, such as the $4,000 School Garden Shelter "given by Mrs. F. F. Thompson." Also funded was an Orchid Greenhouse, for which Daniel Guggenheim and Murry Guggenheim contributed $25,000.

By 1923 the Lorillard mansion had burned, and after discussing the expense of rebuilding it the board voted to demolish what remained. That same year the three parcels of land that the parks department had previously reserved for its own use when it conveyed the additional land in Bronx Park to the Botanical Garden in 1915 were incorporated into the Garden proper. At this point, it was time to review the Garden's landscape in a comprehensive fashion, and the Olmsted Brothers firm was commissioned to prepare a report on its general aesthetics and the scenic success of its component parts. Rightly, the report emphasized the importance of horticultural and grounds maintenance and laid out recommendations for the number of acres to be assigned to employees in various areas of the Garden based on the intensity of care demanded—two to six acres per worker in the highest intensity areas, and six to eighteen acres in the lowest. In all, two and a half times the number of current staff was needed, a recommendation to which Britton acceded.

A large portion of the report concerned circulation within the Garden, and Britton agreed to the improvement of existing features, which included several miles of guardrails on path borders and modern cement surfacing and curbs for drives. But he did not subscribe to the recommendation of rerouting the automobile through-traffic, because, according to his response to the report, "the roads are crowded by motor-cars during only a very small part of the time, estimated at not more than 200 hours during the year." On the other hand, he was in favor of the road proposed to be built across a new bridge below the rapids of the river to connect the Rose Garden and the Iris Garden when funds became available. He endorsed the proposal for a Rhododendron Glade but not the creation of a Model Garden. Where the parks department's greenhouses had been located on the transferred land, he agreed with the recommendation to return this part of the Bronx River valley to essentially its original condition, but he disagreed with the proposed terracing in the Iris Garden region, which he characterized as "a beautiful natural tract, partly forest-enclosed, well adapted to present horticultural usage." Nor did he see the sense of cutting a gap in the woodlands across the rocky ridges to create an east–west vista. The recommended completion of the Garden's boundary wall and fence, however, was for him a clear priority.[13]

In the wake of the Olmsted report a great deal of landscape renovation and enhancement took place. Circulation and infrastructure improvements were made, and Brinley designed additional bridges, entrances, and stairways. During the years of the Great Depression, the Garden was in a state of transition. Britton, whose vision had guided the creation of the Garden over so many years, retired in 1929, and Brinley stepped down as consulting landscape architect in 1931. In 1938 almost a third of the Garden, 120 acres, was sacrificed along the northern and eastern perimeters for the construction of the Bronx River Parkway. In return, the city installed additional fencing along the Garden's borders. Federal relief programs made it possible to employ additional workers to undertake such tasks as clearing, grading, path construction, weeding, and removal of old trees and shrubs.

Amateur gardening was thriving by this time, and with the formation of such organizations as the Horticultural Society of New York and the Garden Club of America, the Garden became even more of a botanical showcase and horticultural learning center for the home gardener during the 1920s and 1930s. Flower collections expanded, and Flower Days featuring single-genera gardens promoted visitation. The landscape designer Ellen Biddle Shipman was hired in 1928 to create a Ladies' Border composed of seasonally blooming bulbs, perennials, and shrubs along the southeast side of the conservatory. The landscape architect Marian Cruger Coffin developed the plan for the installation of the Montgomery Conifer Collection. The British-born horticulturist T. H. Everett, who rose from the position of head gardener to senior curator of education and senior horticulture specialist between 1932 and 1968, designed a new rock garden, later named in his honor.

.

During the twenty-year tenure of William J. Robbins as director beginning in 1938, the Garden responded to the exigencies of World War II with the creation of Victory Gardens on the grounds as well the provision of instruction, information, and publications for the huge number of citizens requesting gardening advice.

William Campbell Steere, a botanist whose specialty, like that of Elizabeth Britton, was bryology, served as the Garden's director and president from 1958 until 1972, when he resumed his career as a scientist. Not surprisingly, the Garden's emphasis during this period was more on field botany and education than on horticulture and grounds beautification.

During Howard Samuel Irwin's directorship, from 1973 until 1979, a long-range plan was set in motion, and the renowned modernist landscape architect Daniel Urban Kiley was responsible for the design of a new entry as well as the Jane Watson Irwin Perennial Garden and the area around the Twin Lakes. Under the administration of James M. Hester, a former president of New York University, who served as director from 1980 until 1989, improvements to the Garden were hampered by New York City's fiscal crisis as well as a shift in budget priorities, causing severe cuts in former municipal support. At this time, increasing public consciousness of threats to the environment stimulated the Garden to take a more active role in examining the effects of pesticides, air pollution, and road salts on plants, as well as unsound forestry practices leading to species extinction. Farrand's beautiful Rose Garden, redesigned by Marian Cruger Coffin in the 1950s, had become defunct during the 1970s. In 1988 it was rebuilt according to Farrand's original design.

But it was not until the period between 1989 and 2018, during which Gregory Long served as the Garden's chief executive officer, that the landscape was fully renewed, along with scientific and educational aims of the institution's mission. During his tenure Long oversaw the preparation of three comprehensive seven-year master plans for the Garden's complete renewal. In addition, he guided their implementation with the same holistic focus as Britton did the original plan. With a background as a professional fundraiser, he was uncommonly successful in attracting private philanthropy, and as a result of new amenities and numerous restorations of both buildings and grounds, visitation dramatically increased.

Among the notable projects accomplished during this period of renaissance are the restoration of the Lord & Burnham conservatory (now named for donor Enid A. Haupt) and the museum building (rechristened the LuEsther T. Mertz Library). Further improvements include the construction of the Garden Café, the Everett Children's Adventure Garden, and the William and Lynda Steere Herbarium.

Building on the popularity of these attractions, the Garden was able to open a new visitor center, the Living Collections glasshouses, and the Pfizer Plant Research Laboratory. At the same time, the grounds were surveyed, mapped, and inventoried. New policies directed toward collections management were instituted, and the three-and-a-half-acre Native Plant Garden, made possible by a $15 million gift from the Leon Levy Foundation, was opened; the two-and-a-half-acre Rock Garden was restored; Farrand's Rose Garden (now named for Peggy Rockefeller) was replanted; the Benenson Ornamental Conifers collection was installed nearby; and the original pinetum next to the conservatory was revised and renamed the Arthur and Janet Ross Conifer Arboretum. Ongoing outreach efforts under the Garden's current president, Carrie Rebora Barratt, include an environmental program called Bronx Green-up and science curricula development for teachers. Scientists continue to do research abroad. In addition to the earlier purposes of botanical discovery and taxonomy, the emphasis is now on studying plant biodiversity and the effects of ecosystem destruction and climate change. Specimens from field expeditions are stored in the Steere Herbarium and their digitized images and data made universally accessible on the Internet.

.

Looking back over more than a century since the New York Botanical Garden was founded, we can see that its existence was due to a propitious constellation of forces—available land, capital resources, and the visionary leadership of its founders and their successors. Most of the documents chronicling its creation and construction can be found in the archives of the Mertz Library. By observing this great New York City institution come into existence and its landscape develop according to the plans drawn by Vaux and Parsons, Brinley, Farrand, and later designers while at the same time researching the actions, events, decision-making processes, and fundraising efforts that were responsible for its creation, revision, and renewal, one comes to the conclusion that the New York Botanical Garden has succeeded and even surpassed its original creators' ambition to create "an American Kew."

Representing Nature

The Dioramas of the American Museum of Natural History

(2013)

When we think of landscape as an art form we tend to think of painting. In this case the names Claude Lorrain, John Constable, and Jean-Baptiste-Camille Corot come to mind, along with American artists of the Hudson River School such as Thomas Cole, Albert Bierstadt, Asher Durand, and Frederic Church. But who recalls the names of Frank Chapman and Carl Akeley? And yet, for the past century, hundreds of thousands of adults and children have observed their three-dimensional landscapes with curiosity and wonder—those exhibitions of birds and mammals from Asia, Africa, and North America that are displayed in replicas of their native settings in several lofty halls of the American Museum of Natural History. Seen through frames of glass, these illuminated animals are not only set against painted landscapes but also surrounded by actual plants or highly realistic simulacra, as well as rocks and stones gleaned from specific sites or fabricated when originals were too large to collect.

Chapman and Akeley were the esteemed pioneers of this exhibition technique, and their collaborators and followers—William R. Leigh, Robert Rockwell, James Perry Wilson, Belmore Browne, Francis Lee Jaques, and Robert Kane—furthered the museum's reputation as the premier institution committed to this type of display.

From *Site/Lines* 8.2 (Spring 2013).

The descendants of cycloramas—360-degree panoramic paintings of important sites and historical events mounted on the inside of cylindrical drums—and of Louis Daguerre's theatrically backlit scrims giving painted scenery an illusion of spatial depth, habitat dioramas portray natural specimens in three-dimensional settings of great verisimilitude. This lineage begs a further question: are habitat dioramas science or art?

Stephen Quinn, who has helped to conserve and create them for the past thirty-nine years in the Exhibition Department of the museum, believes they are both. Quinn considers Chapman and Akeley masters of this form of landscape depiction, which fuses sculpture, painting, and collage in compositions of extraordinary fidelity. For him these men are revered progenitors, great naturalists who were explorers, specimen collectors, and taxidermists all in one. The fact that they bagged their quarry with a gun, just as Audubon killed his subjects in order to accurately draw and paint them for *The Birds of America,* is not a problem for him. "Whether bird or mammal, all the specimens in dioramas have necessarily been collected in the wild by men who were good shots," he told me, as we stood in front of the magnificent diorama of a herd of bison in the recently restored Bernard Family Hall of North American Mammals. "These were not hunters for sport. Rather they were scientists with an important conservation message, early defenders of the world's vanishing, pristine landscapes—particularly the wildlife habitats in America and Africa that in the early twentieth century were seriously endangered by wealthy sportsmen, food harvesters, and plume hunters—much as they are today by clear-cutting, natural-resource extraction, and overdevelopment. This is what the American Museum of Natural History was all about from the beginning—collecting wildlife and creating displays to show people the wonders of nature and wake them up to the fact that a lot of it was in danger of being lost."

After mid-twentieth-century modernism cast a cold eye on representational art, and as wildlife films and television shows became popular, some discredited the museum's dioramas as outdated—a position Quinn has always strongly opposed. On the contrary, he staunchly maintains that the three-dimensionality of these lifelike and life-size animal forms renders them more emotionally compelling than animals seen on television or computer screen. He firmly believes that the sophisticated techniques that provide illusory spatial breadth and depth give the dioramas much more verisimilitude than their photographic counterparts.

Quinn also believes that the dioramas' re-creations of specific settings, inhabited by creatures most people will never see in the wild, are compelling testaments to nature's sublimity—and a visceral means of educating the museum's five million annual visitors about the importance of landscape conservation. According to him, the conservation ethos of the museum is built into the institution's DNA; by the end of the nineteenth century, not only the great diorama artists but also the museum's science curators and philanthropic supporters were viewing vanishing wildlife species with justifiable concern. "The passenger pigeon was rapidly becoming extinct," he explained. "Game birds for the table were being shot in vast numbers, the railroads had turned buffalo hunting into a sport, and the market for plumes for the millinery trade caused the slaughter of hundreds of thousands of egrets, flamingos, and other shore birds."

Then, in 1885 Morris K. Jesup, third president of the museum, traveled to London and saw the mounted bird specimens in the British Museum. "Upon his return," Quinn said, "he found a dedicated young ornithologist—Frank Chapman—and hired him to collect birds within a fifty-mile radius of New York City. This was the beginning of our earliest dioramas. Come, I'll take you upstairs to see the Hall of North American Birds." There he showed me several of Chapman's early efforts in a series of four-sided glass cases containing mounted bird specimens and botanical models, which at first appeared to be three-dimensional versions of Audubon paintings of birds exquisitely posed on the branches of botanically interesting plants. Quinn described how Chapman had later improved his displays by adding curved backdrop panels with paintings depicting the original habitats from which the specimens had been collected. Moreover, he brought artists with him into the field in order to portray the landscapes they encountered as accurately as possible.

Chapman went on to create window-protected, stage-style dioramas, the earliest being the one of Florida's Pelican Island constructed in 1902. Quinn noted, "He chose this subject because the pelican was one of the many water birds that were on the brink of extinction. Plume hunters would lie in wait in the mangroves near their nests so that they could kill them when they came in to feed their young. As president at the time, Theodore Roosevelt, a naturalist himself and son of one of the founders of the museum, was able to get Congress to enact legislation in 1903 designating Pelican Island the first federal bird reserve." Much to Quinn's regret, the Pelican Island diorama was destroyed when Chapman's original Hall of North American Birds was modernized in the 1960s.

Quinn himself is widely considered to be one of the most expert birders in the region, and the museum-sponsored bird walks he leads in the Central Park Ramble during the May migration season have a large following. His ornithological skills were honed when he was a boy growing up in Ridgefield Park, New Jersey. He credits his parents with sharing their reverence for nature with their children, taking them on vacations to national parks and other wilderness areas. Even more formative for his career as a naturalist and avian expert was his older brother, who took him on many adventurous explorations of the Hackensack Meadows next to their home. "In those days it was a paradise," he recalled. "For me it was just like being Tom Sawyer. On Saturdays we would go out early in the morning on rafts, and I would help my brother collect birds for the aviary and ponds he kept in the back yard. Sometimes we would filch one or two eggs from a nest, incubate them in a warm place at home, and then raise the chicks. Of course, it is completely illegal nowadays to keep wild birds, and even at that time the game warden would occasionally pay us a visit. Then when my brother got his driver's license, whenever we read about an oil spill in the newspapers, we would go patrol the beaches and run into the surf and catch ducks. After we brought them home, our mom would let us wash them in the bathtub."

And then there was the American Museum of Natural History. "It was just thrilling to climb those grand steps and walk into the Theodore Roosevelt Rotunda," he said. "It was like being in St. Paul's Cathedral or some other great religious space. You could say that this place was the temple where I worshipped nature. After I graduated from Ridgefield Park High School, my guidance counselor directed me into a career in wildlife management. Since I had been painting and sketching my entire life until then, I decided to transfer to the Ridgewood School of Art and Design. When I graduated in 1974, as luck would have it, the New York State Council on the Arts was sponsoring an internship program that had been started here at the museum. Even though dioramas were somewhat out of fashion at that time, it was a farsighted way for the museum to train a new generation of diorama artists, since the old ones were all gone or about to retire."

.

Chapman's creation of the Hall of North American Birds provided only a sample of what lay ahead in the museum's development of the diorama as its principal mode of natural-history education. It was Carl Akeley who, by combining the skills of a sculptor, a naturalist, an explorer, and a taxidermist, brought this art form into its golden age after the museum's fourth president, Henry Fairfield Osborn, hired him away from the Field Museum in Chicago in 1909. There he had perfected what came to be known as the Akeley technique, a lifelike presentation method he had earlier demonstrated with the creation of a relatively small muskrat diorama. Now, with Osborn's support, he was ready to apply his skills to the mounting of two fighting bull elephants. As Quinn ushered me downstairs to the Akeley Hall of African Mammals, he extolled its namesake's unsurpassed prowess as the creator of dioramas.

When I asked him to describe the process of creating the taxidermic specimens on display, Quinn explained how Akeley took extensive field measurements, modeled clay around a skeletal armature to create a detailed sculpture of the animal, and then covered the clay with the beast's stripped hide, which had been processed at a tannery to make it supple and insect-proof. But this was not the end of the process. Quinn went on to describe how the wet clay within the now skin-clothed animal would have been further manipulated by Akeley to ensure a subtler detailing of the musculature, wrinkles, and folds, and to perfect the lifelike pose he had conceived for the manikin. When Akeley was satisfied, a plaster cast was made that encased the entire hide-covered clay sculpture. Once hardened, the plaster and underlying pelt were incised and separated into two halves. The hard clay was then removed from these molds and the skeleton sent back to the Department of Mammalogy, after which Akeley's team filled the plaster shells with papier-mâché. Once it was dry, they reunited the two halves of this cast, removed the plaster from the exterior, sewed the skin together again at the seams, and concealed the marks of the stitching.

This revelation took me a moment to absorb. "Do you mean," I asked, "that these huge elephants are lightweights—just papier-mâché figures with hides covering them?" "Yes," Quinn replied, "they weigh a lot less than an actual elephant, but they are very sturdy. There is a picture of Akeley riding on top of one."

The centerpiece of the Hall of African Mammals is a freestanding herd of eight elephants that includes a cow elephant collected by Theodore Roosevelt and a calf collected by his son Kermit on an African safari in 1909 at the same time that Akeley was leading an expedition for the museum. Thanks to Roosevelt's donation of his and Kermit's elephants, Akeley was able to unite them with the two bull elephants he had previously collected and mounted and present the four in a grouping called "The Alarm," which was placed on exhibit in a hall named the Akeley Elephant Room. The splendid Hall of African Mammals where they now stand would not open until 1936, ten years after Akeley's death. At that time, four other elephants collected by the museum's fifth president, F. Trubee Davison, were added to the group.

The story behind this multi-animal grouping testifies to the courage of naturalist collectors who were willing to risk their lives in pursuit of dangerous creatures. In Akeley's case, vision and tenacity were involved as well. Near the end of his 1909 African expedition, while shooting photographs in the bamboo forest on the lower slopes of Mount Kenya, he was charged and mauled by a rogue elephant. It was while he was still in the field during months spent convalescing from this almost fatal accident that he conceived of the Hall of African Mammals. Back at the museum and on subsequent expeditions to Africa, he dedicated the rest of his career to its realization. Although Akeley did not live to see it completed, the grand Hall of African Mammals—with its forty-foot-high ceilings, handsome Art Deco architectural detailing, and twenty-eight illuminated diorama encasements encircling the ground floor and mezzanine—is in accord with the scheme he had envisioned. The freestanding elephant grouping at its center, which is visible from the Theodore Roosevelt Rotunda at the museum's main entrance on 79th Street and Central Park West, can be considered to be the institution's iconic heart. Although some curators have disagreed, Quinn believes that the room should remain dimly lit, like a theater, with its walls of serpentine—a dark green stone composed of ferromagnesian minerals—free of labels, so that the dioramas are always the principal focus of the visitor's attention.

When I asked Quinn which of Akeley's dioramas in this hall was his favorite, he took me over to the window in front of the mountain gorilla specimens. Akeley had collected them in 1921 in the rainforests of Mount Mikeno among the Kivu volcanoes in the region of what was then the Belgian Congo. "Remember," Quinn said, "Akeley and the other scientists of this museum were Darwinians. They understood the kinship between gorillas and human beings. Akeley even wrote of the remorse he experienced when he killed the great silverback gorilla you see here. He called it 'a magnificent beast with the face of an amiable giant who would do no harm' and said he felt like a murderer. And because of the beautiful surroundings, he said that he 'envied this chap his funeral pyre.'"

In order to ensure that the diorama's background would appear as site-specific as possible, Akeley returned to the Mount Mikeno region in 1926 with an accomplished plein-air landscape painter of the American West, William R. Leigh. To achieve an equally realistic foreground he brought along staff to collect the botanical specimens that would serve as models for their fabricated counterparts. It was at this time that Akeley fell gravely ill and died. Fittingly, the intrepid explorer-cum–wildlife artist was buried on the site, which was the place he had declared the most beautiful on earth.

In November 2010, Quinn visited the region on another museum expedition to create a series of paintings—this time for the purpose of pairing recent images with the diorama in New York in order to document the environmental changes that have occurred in the area around Mount Mikeno where tropical sublimity has been compromised by clear-cutting on the slopes and the green valley visible in the diorama has been parceled into agricultural fields. Many of these are now used as encampments for refugees who have been displaced by the ongoing war and civil unrest in the Democratic Republic of the Congo and Rwanda. "You see," Quinn concluded, "a large number of the dioramas here at the museum serve as records of various landscapes as they were before human intervention and disturbance. Today, when there are no more than an estimated seven hundred mountain gorillas left in the world, this is how we can remember what their habitats once were and understand why we should preserve the remaining ones like them."

As we moved downstairs to the Hall of North American Mammals, I asked Quinn about the other taxidermists, background painters, and foreground specialists who had helped to create the museum's fascinating windows on nature. To introduce me to another of the diorama artists who are his heroes, Quinn took me to the mule deer diorama painted by James Perry Wilson, whom he considers to be the most important background painter of all time. Wilson, who started his career in the museum under the tutelage of William R. Leigh in the Hall of African Mammals, developed a method that took into account perspectival optics. Previously it had been a matter of guesswork for an artist to compensate graphically for the inevitable distortions that occur when a flat image is transferred to a curved surface by means of a regular orthogonal grid. Wilson, however, who had trained as an architect, developed a grid that he was able to geometrically alter in such a way that its squares change in size and shape toward the edges of the diorama's curved background wall, while the view remains realistically perspectival when viewed from a central position.

Before plotting the diorama's background scenery according to his manipulated grid, Wilson used panoramic stereoscopic photographs as references in placing the horizon line at exactly five feet two inches from the ground, which he considered to be the average viewing height of a museum visitor. If all this sounds overly mechanical, one must recall that Renaissance painters also manipulated the lines of conventional grids in order to accurately capture perspective in the cartoons they created as underdrawings for paintings. More important, as Quinn explained to me, once Wilson had sketched a diorama's background scenery according to his mathematically formulated grid, he referred back to his plein-air paintings to ensure that their color tones and values approached those seen by the naked eye when looking into the distance outdoors.

In the manner of an art historian, Quinn analyzed Wilson's technique. Viewing the mule deer diorama with the butte called Devil's Tower in the background, I could appreciate the subtle gradations in the sky from the acme to the horizon line, and the way in which the artist used a weaker chroma to convey the haziness of the distant mountain ridge and the pinkish amber light of late afternoon. Quinn pointed out that the matte surface made the scene more naturalistic since paint mixed with medium is too glossy to create a totally realistic impression, adding that Wilson never used blacks because he could achieve more nuanced tones by mixing complementary colors. It was through these techniques that Wilson increased his paintings' verisimilitude.

The trickiest part of diorama creation may be seamlessly melding the painted background into the arranged foreground with its real or artificial plants, rocks, grass, gravel, sand, or snow in a tableau in which the lifelike taxidermic animal sculptures are the star attraction. Beyond this, the hues, values, and directional illumination of the background painting must be consonant with the three-dimensional foreground objects, so that there is a unified perspective with no apparent dividing line between front and back.

"Lighting is a critical factor," Quinn told me. "Getting the electrical light source—which is concealed the same way that stage lights are in a theater—evenly directed and dispersed so that background and foreground appear to share the same time of day is important. There can't be any hot spots, and the whole scene has to be illuminated in a way that makes the light appear to be coming from one side. Here in the mule deer diorama you can see by the background sky and how the light falls across the landscape that the time of day is late afternoon. Look at the way it illuminates Devil's Tower in the background and how the foreground shadows are all in the same direction."

Just on the other side of the plate-glass window a doe was grazing, and an antlered male was looking about alertly, as if aware of our presence. On the realistic gravel- and grass-covered ground near their feet, I saw that the shadows corresponded perfectly with the slant of the light source. Quinn explained, "Some shadowy tones had to also be painted into the vegetation in the foreground in order to get just the right effect of reflected light in the outdoors." Returning to the American bison and pronghorn antelope diorama—the largest in the museum—I could see how Wilson and his apprentice Fred Scherer, with the help of mammalogist T. Donald Carter and foreground artist George Peterson, had managed to achieve similar effects by the same means on an even grander scale.

As we circled around the perimeter gallery in the Hall of North American Mammals, we stopped by another Wilson masterpiece, the wolf diorama. Standing in front of this nocturnal snow scene, Quinn pointed out Wilson's understanding of meteorology and astronomy as well as nighttime light. "You can see the luminous streaks of the aurora borealis, and there is Polaris and the constellations in exactly the positions they occupied at 3 a.m. on December 7, 1941, when observed from the place where Wilson stood in a forest somewhere between Minnesota and Ontario, painting his background sketch."

Quinn called my attention to other accurately studied details. "Notice how the shadows of the two running wolves were fabricated by the foreground artist Raymond deLucia, who sprinkled dry color onto the artificial snow, which is made from marble dust and sparkling mica chips. That is because the low-level fluorescent lamps with blue filters used to simulate nocturnal light are incapable of casting shadows in this scene. You can see that the dry-color shadows fall according to the position of the full moon, which can't be seen but can be imagined to be somewhere outside the diorama.

"Now look at the wolves' tracks in the snow, and you will see how accurately they depict the way a wolf runs at high speed. This is called a 'gathered suspension'—the point in each sequence of strides when all four feet are off the ground and gathered below the animal." Quinn then pointed out a different set of tracks, also apparently made at top speed but with all four feet outstretched for the next stride, the resulting pattern indicating an animal that runs with an "extended" suspension. "Now these are the kind of footprints that show exactly the way the tracks of a white-tail deer fleeing from its predator would appear," he explained. "A lot of people who see these dioramas won't notice such things, but this is what makes them valid in the eyes of the naturalists who come here to study them."

For Quinn, however, there is also a moral—and even a religious—dimension to his work. He firmly believes that in our homocentric era of global transformation and climate change the museum's dioramas are testaments to nature's divinity, echoing Thoreau's dictum that "in wildness is the preservation of the world." Their scientific accuracy, combined with exquisite craftsmanship, is what makes them so morally instructive. "Now that there are tremendous threats to biodiversity and habitat destruction going on all around us," he said, "visitors to this museum can see how beautiful these places are, or once were. You can't destroy nature heedlessly; these creatures and we are part of a single web of life on this planet."

PART II

Along the Shoreline

On Phillip Lopate's

Waterfront: A Journey around Manhattan

(2005)

There is a genre of writing that can be called "On the Road" lit-erature. It often attempts to portray the enigmatic ordinary of Elsewhere in a series of trenchant, if necessarily superficial, obser-vations. Writers of this genre are almost always intellectually curi-ous outsiders with a wandering bent who bring a sharp eye, ear, and journalistic voice to their travels. Photographers hit the road for the same purpose, sometimes producing indelibly memorable, culture-defining images. Still, there are pitfalls here. Within the seemingly dispassionate writer's pen or photographer's lens lurk preconceived political positions and an inevitable, if unconscious, sense of superiority, which even the most sympathetic artists and writers have toward their subjects simply because they are in con-trol of the presentation of their material.

In *Waterfront: A Journey around Manhattan,* Phillip Lopate has chosen a more restricted compass and an approach that is both more tentative and more deeply exploratory than that of the usual "On the Road" author. He is not a motorcycle or automobile man streaking across the highways of America, interviewing cattle ranchers, barflies, trailer-park residents, marine reservists, and gas station attendants. He is, first and foremost, a son of the city (New York City, of course), an inveterate urban walker, a latter-day fla-

Book review, *New Criterion* 23.9 (May 2005).

neur, and a master of the personal essay whose sensibility leads him into meditative byways derived from a pedestrian's perspective on diverse local identities.

Lopate has two other taut strings in his literary bow: He is an anthologist and an aficionado of film. His first anthology, *The Art of the Personal Essay* (1994), reflects his familiarity with the literary form he has appropriated as his own, and his second, *Writing New York* (1998), makes handy for recall a rich body of the city's waterfront literature. Linking word and place, he can summon at will lines of Walt Whitman and Hart Crane, refer to the lurid and tantalizing plethora of nineteenth-century "Lights and Shadows" books that sensationalized New York's high and low life, or heighten our social awareness of the past with incidents drawn from Jacob Riis's *How the Other Half Lives* (1890) or Herbert Asbury's *The Gangs of New York* (1928). As someone whose lifelong passion for the movies has yielded a body of reviews and essays on the subject of film, he sees street life cinematically and remembers the streets of the city (or the Hollywood set designs of them) in all their moody film-noir glory and Woody Allen satirical charm.

As Lopate points out, most of our solitary walks take place not only on the pavement but also in our heads, as our thoughts shuttle back and forth between self-absorption and observation. It is good, therefore, to find ourselves in the company of such a well-furnished mind as his and to know that all the seeing and learning and remembering that are stored there will come to us as the same kind of interior monologue we would like to have with ourselves—pondering some flash of beauty or decrepitude, some piece of history or personal memory, some missed opportunity or qualified urban planning success—if we only had in our heads so much lightly worn historical research, so many behind-the-scenes interviews, such quick recall of great old movies and passages from hundreds of books about New York. Moreover, it is good to be reminded that we all see the world idiosyncratically and to realize that, if we live long enough in as restless a city as New York, the scenery of our past and present walks in the same neighborhoods will become increasingly disassociated through change.

Nowhere is urban flux more evident than on Manhattan's twenty-first-century waterfront. Not only in New York but in many formerly important port and manufacturing cities, industrial lands adjacent to shorelines and river docks have become "brownfields," contaminated sites that now present an opportunity for revitalization. And nowhere is the opportunity to renew the urban edge more potently dramatic or more fraught with political and bureaucratic obstacles than in New York.

In his self-assigned task of exploring on foot as much of the Manhattan waterfront as possible, Lopate tells us, "All along, I kept coming up against certain underlying questions: What is our capacity for city-making at this historical juncture? How did we formerly build cities with such casual conviction, and can we still come up with bold, integrated visions and ambitious works? What is the changing meaning of public space? How to resolve the anti-urban bias in our national character with the need to sustain a vital city environment? Or reconcile New York's past as a port/manufacturing center with the new model of a postindustrial city given over to information processing and consumerism?"

While these pressing issues engage Lopate's attention, *Waterfront* is anything but a prescriptive book. Like Baudelaire or Walter Benjamin before him, Lopate's real métier is walking to write, a desire to sample the pleasures and perils of modernity with a sensibility attuned to history, to experiencing what he calls "the ever-enigmatic, alien fusion of presence and absence." He is, in other words, a connoisseur of how the transformation of cities by industrial, and now postindustrial, forces is played out in the lives and visages and words of casually encountered strangers. At the same time, he sees the waterfront as an anthology of past lives and a palimpsest of past places. It is a landscape that he has tried to read like a history book, conjuring the stevedores and the sailors, the gamins and the grit, the factories and the foghorns. Pulling himself up short of sentimentality, Lopate often writes his then-and-now passages in a tone of nostalgia, which he justifies when he remarks, "The walker-writer cannot help seeing, superimposed over the present edifice, its former incarnation, and he/she sings the necropolis."

In *Waterfront* we follow Lopate first up Manhattan's Hudson River shoreline from the Battery to Washington Heights and Inwood Hill and then from the Battery to Highbridge Park along the East River as he traces the present shoreline and its bordering neighborhoods, regarding them as layered accumulations of older narratives. Though its cacophonous vibrancy is stilled, his Manhattan waterfront is yet haunted by colorful, if continually fading, ghosts.

Lopate thus calls attention to the comparative vacancy of the once busy harbor as abandoned piers rot or, as he explains in one fascinating chapter, are eaten away by shipworms. Always, we see tantalizing opportunity for waterfront "reclamation" being tortuously realized or just out of reach of political will and economic viability as we follow Lopate's physical and intellectual perambulations. Because *Waterfront* is personal in its perspective, one has to recognize the author's penchant for the vulgar, seedy, and picturesquely decrepit: the "rotting timbers, tall grass, jagged rocks, and wharfside warehouses which constituted the 1970–1980s New York waterfront, after it had been given up as a port but before it had begun to be 'rehabilitated.'"

Even prior to this, the waterfront had become a kind of abstraction, devoid of almost all of its old marine traffic and commerce and sealed off from physical contact by highways. At best (and indeed a blessing under the circumstances), it could be viewed from a high promenade such as the one on the deck built over the FDR Drive as it passes beneath the grounds of Gracie Mansion and Carl Schurz Park. Only in a few marginal places such as East Harlem can you thread your way through riprap, rusty fences, and high weeds alongside the water's edge.

It is not, however, precisely this "ragged, unkempt, undiscovered, and unidentified territory" that, sore of foot and leg, Lopate prescribes as an antidote to the manicured edge represented by the Battery Park Promenade. What frustrates him are the too-timid official planning visions and bland consumer-oriented public space improvements prevalent nowadays. He longs for an older, crustier reality that somehow acknowledges the vanished dockworkers and harbor traffic—but without turning the waterfront into self-themed, commercially driven historic districts, as in the case of South Street Seaport. But none of us knows how to summon an economically defunct past without having it seem like a staged revival. At best, one can join Lopate in applauding the kind of vigilante urbanism exercised by communities that give up on government and improve derelict public spaces on their own.

Shoreline meditation gives rise here and there to an excursus or digression. These chapters constitute thematic essays of a historical or biographical nature, thus differing from the more purely descriptive ones elsewhere. For me, the most telling of these literary detours is the story of the bitterly fought and defeated plan to replace Manhattan's West Side Highway with Westway, a planned shoreline transportation corridor submerged in the Hudson River that would have been decked over with several hundred acres of parkland. Lopate explains how this proposal would have reconnected the city's street grid with its waterfront, making the Hudson between 79th Street and the Battery as accessible as it is above 79th Street in the neighborhoods adjacent to Riverside Park. Yet it was killed after a protracted fight that pitted community activists and highway transportation planners against one another.

Lopate helps us see in hindsight how Westway fell victim to historical timing. In the late 1960s, when this project was on the drawing boards, federal funding was available. But in the early 1970s, as lawsuits to block Westway were wending their way through the courts, any Robert Moses–style top-down urban planning project had become de facto suspect, and newly established community planning boards were finding their principal political power to lie in opposition to large-scale, government-sponsored urban renewal. For more than a decade, opponents fought the project, at last triumphing on environmental grounds. Their case, which was upheld in court, was based on the importance of the Hudson estuary as a breeding habitat for striped bass.

Now, thirty years later, instead of the large park that would have united the riverfront with its adjacent inland neighborhoods, Route 9A—a rebuilt West Side Highway in the guise of a wide boulevard—

continues to separate them from the bikeway and recreational pier projects that are gradually aggregating as state funding becomes available. Such is Lopate's revisionist take on the project that he, like many other New Yorkers including myself, opposed at the time.

This affinity for planning analysis, combined with a sensory appreciation of Manhattan's old waterfront landscape—a description of what was, is, might have been, and is coming into being in this most incessantly self-transforming of cities—makes Lopate's book more original, balanced, and nuanced than others on the subject. It is hard to say which of the personal essays that constitute *Waterfront* is best. The entire circuit that this walker in the city makes around Manhattan's waterfront, narrated as the story of one man's love affair with the greatest city on earth and the incomparable estuarine harbor that set its dynamic development in motion, is fascinating and timely.

Beneath the Great Bridge

A Park Grows in Brooklyn

(2000–2001)

The magnetism of the water's edge is compelling; people gravitate to lands' ends. So when the waterside becomes a recreational frontage, it is bound to attract visitors. Reclaiming and stitching together transformed shoreline "brownfields"—shaggy remains of defunct factories—and uniting them with already existing publicly accessible sites along the waterfront is one way to create new urban bikeways, jogging trails, and promenades.

In the eyes of the conservationists and park planners who would revitalize destroyed ecosystems and provide needed amenities, brownfields are the green fields of the future. The clean air and water movement, which helped create antipollution legislation to reverse the degradation of rivers, bays, and streams, has made these near-abandoned landscapes viable sites for river- and harbor-related parks. Such born-again postindustrial landscapes at the water's edge are key elements in the current trend toward urban revitalization, especially when they are physically and visually connected to the surrounding cityscape, even though separated from it by highways, rail lines, or other formidable barriers to access.

New York City's growth to commercial greatness was based on its incomparable harbor, but since that geophysical and historic asset no longer drives the city's economy as it once did, the Port

From *Cityscape Institute News,* Winter 2000–2001.

Authority of New York and New Jersey has been able to declare several Manhattan and Brooklyn piers surplus real estate. These port-related brownfields offer an unprecedented opportunity for creating several continuous strips of waterside recreation, especially when their conversion is combined with the renewal of aging nearby waterfront parks. The creation of Hudson River Park and the proposed promenades and playing fields on Governors Island are examples of this large-scale, ongoing waterfront reclamation effort. The current revitalization of badly deteriorated Battery Park and the parklands along the Harlem and Bronx Rivers also typify this trend, due in large measure to organized efforts spearheaded by private support groups, in these cases the Battery Conservancy, the New York Restoration Project, and the Bronx River Restoration Project.

The Port Authority's release for sale of five Brooklyn piers that are no longer needed for shipping has presented the city with an especially magnificent opportunity to turn brownfields into green fields. Here, crouched beneath the soaring rusticated stone pylons of the Brooklyn Bridge and with a panoramic perspective of lower Manhattan's constellated towers and the Statue of Liberty, a seventy-acre site with one of America's noblest and most historic waterfront views is poised for recreational rebirth. Thanks to public officials—notably Mayor Rudolph Giuliani, Brooklyn borough president Howard Golden, New York City Council speaker Peter Vallone, and council members Kenneth Fisher and Herb Berman—$63.5 million in New York City capital budget funding has recently been committed and another $75 million is being sought from New York State to realize a visionary effort begun a number of years ago.

Like many large visions, the one for the proposed $150 million park sprouted because an earlier seed of optimistic enterprise had germinated in the alien soil of the same brownfield, or rather the water of New York Harbor. That seed consisted of an old barge once used by the Erie Lackawanna Railroad and converted in 1977 into a floating performance space for chamber music concerts. Its owner is Bargemusic, the nonprofit organization created by Olga Bloom, a violinist who wanted to give young musicians the oppor-

tunity to perform chamber concerts in a compelling setting that
would attract small appreciative audiences. Nearby, the River Café,
a haute-cuisine restaurant built on the same premise that a romantically breathtaking view would be a potent draw for patrons, also
opened in 1977. With these trailblazers well established by the mid-
1990s, the New York City Economic Development Corporation
undertook the $4 million redevelopment of historic Fulton Ferry
Landing between the River Café and Bargemusic.

Today it is hard to remember that the site of landscape architect Signe Nielsen's award-winning design for that project, with
its handsome decking inset with bronze historic-map medallions,
high-grade marine stainless steel railings echoing the diagonal
splay of the bridge cables above, and railing panels incised with
lines from Walt Whitman's "Crossing Brooklyn Ferry" was previously sealed off to the public by rusty chain-link fencing. In
addition to forming a pleasing connection between River Café
and Bargemusic, Fulton Ferry Landing hosts a seemingly endless
weekend parade of bridal parties arriving in white limousines,
with photographers in tow to capture for posterity the significance
of the nuptial occasion by recording it against the backdrop of the
iconic bridge.

·

The campaign for a park running north and south of Fulton Ferry
Landing was begun approximately fifteen years ago by a group of
community residents. Out of this initiative on the part of private
citizens, the Brooklyn Bridge Park Coalition was formed in 1989
to advocate and develop a plan for a world-class park on the downtown Brooklyn waterfront. The coalition, which is comprised of
sixty civic, environmental, and cultural groups and more than a
thousand individual members, has steadily built the political and
community consensus that is critical to the realization of a public
space project of such magnitude. To achieve this, it commissioned
leading designers to develop a conceptual plan for a park extending from Atlantic Avenue northward to the Manhattan Bridge and
including the Port Authority's Piers 1 through 5 as well as the exist-

ing Empire–Fulton Ferry State Park located in the "inter-bridge" area between the Brooklyn and Manhattan Bridges.

In 1999 the designated developer of city-owned lots in the area revealed a plan for a 376,000-square-foot hotel and multiplex retail center that would have reduced open space and obstructed the site's bridge, water, and skyline views. In addition, its bulky footprint and sleek postmodernist design were considerably at odds with the scale and architectural texture of its surroundings, notably the block of historic nineteenth-century brick warehouses known as the Empire Stores.

The Brooklyn Bridge Park Coalition, which opposed the plan, succeeded in getting it shelved while developing an alternative community-based proposal for the site. Al Butzel, a veteran environmentalist and founder of the Hudson River Alliance, became president of the coalition in 1999, adding his experience in campaigning for waterfront parks to the effective leadership of executive director Tensie Whelan and her successor, Marianna Koval.

Thanks in large part to the coalition's work over the past decade, what was once a concept on the part of citizens for the creation of Brooklyn Bridge Park has evolved into a commitment by state and city officials. In 1998 the Brooklyn Bridge Park Development Corporation (BBPDC) was chartered by the New York State legislature and Department of State to undertake planning for the area between the Brooklyn-Queens Expressway and the waterfront from Atlantic Avenue to Brooklyn Bridge, the site of the soon-to-be-decommissioned Port Authority piers.

With $1.9 million in state funds, the BBPDC, led by president Joanne Witty and a board of civic representatives, business leaders, and public officials, hired a team of urban planning consultants to study the site and make recommendations concerning the nature of the park-to-be. The coalition is headed by John Alschuler of Hamilton, Rabinovitz & Alschuler, a firm specializing in project management and economic development analysis, and includes the architect Ken Greenberg of Urban Strategies in Toronto and the Cambridge and New York City landscape architect Michael Van Valkenburgh.

When the BBPDC's planning mandate was subsequently expanded north to the Manhattan Bridge, the coalition, which had hired Raymond Gindroz of Urban Design Associates to develop a community-based proposal for the inter-bridge area, contributed his services as a consultant to the planning team. In addition, the BBPDC embraced the coalition's concept of a community design-participation process. To date, more than three thousand people have attended dozens of meetings, including a series of workshops in which the planning team has encouraged community members to identify constraints and opportunities, listened to priorities and ideas, and responded with design alternatives. Recognizing that participatory planning is an iterative process, the team structured the workshops to provide a sequential series of opportunities for discussion, presentation, review, and revision.

The complexity of the design development of the 1.3-mile-long, 75-acre site and achieving a consensus among the diversity of the constituencies it will serve in order to guarantee that Brooklyn Bridge Park will be a public space combining several different environments and recreational uses is challenging. To facilitate the community's dialogue about the opportunities and constraints of the site, the BBPDC-designated project designer, Michael Van Valkenburgh, developed a rubric of four landscape types. These include:

Natural: Composed of self-sustaining native ecosystems rich in opportunity for environmental education, this type of landscape boasts wetland grasses and rock-rimmed coves that serve as habitats for birds and marine wildlife.

Boundless: Olmstedian in concept, this landscape type is characterized by expansive openness and breadth of views, thereby creating a sense of limitless space and stirring poetic imagination.

Civic: Programmed as comfortable, sociable spaces, the civic landscape is specifically designed as a gathering place where people can sit, play sports, picnic, and enjoy the outdoors and companionship of one another.

Urban: Conceived as busy public spaces filled with the movement of people, this kind of landscape consists of plazas and streetscapes that link the park with the surrounding city and nearby recreational and cultural facilities.

By layering the opportunities explored with the community on top of the constraints presented by the site and then factoring neighbors' concerns into an iterative planning process, the consultants have produced a cohesive vision for the park that embodies all of these premises for its design. It is a vision that maximizes views of the skyline, the harbor, and the Manhattan and Brooklyn Bridges, providing new ways to enjoy the historic site and experience the water's edge. It also creates flexible open space to accommodate a range of outdoor activities, while at the same time enabling users to experience the park as a whole by establishing a "continuous ribbon" of pedestrian and bicycle paths along its length. It offers physical and visual connections to the surrounding blocks that do not currently exist. In specific terms, it prescribes an enlarged wetland cove in the inter-bridge zone, a walled garden and a café within the picturesque old structure of the Empire Stores, a special place for skateboarders under the noisy Manhattan Bridge, an open-air market near Fulton Ferry Landing, a marina between Piers 1 and 2, an amphitheater and a fountain on Pier 3, and a number of other sports and recreation facilities placed strategically throughout the park.

If the promise of this plan is realized through thoughtful implementation and overarching vision, careful attention to detail, and responsible management, the seed of an idea that took root on the decaying piers in the shadow of the Brooklyn Bridge and was nurtured by dedicated citizens and public officials through the pitfalls of politics and the realities of economics will have grown into one of the greatest urban waterfront parks of the twenty-first century. Clearly, for New York City and the borough of Brooklyn, the waterfront is where the new millennium begins.

On New York's Aged Waterfront, a Pinch of Salt

(1971)

Below the great Gothic pylons and harp strings of the Brooklyn Bridge lies Manhattan's South Street. In the age of sail, South Street was a synonym for the Port of New York, but nowadays lower Manhattan is ringed with abandoned piers. By all odds South Street would appear doomed, a victim of the New York City game called Real Estate Dynamics. The trend is clear: the old small-scale industries are dying or moving elsewhere as land values continue to escalate and towering office buildings are usurping their sites on the urban chessboard. But a curious confluence of energy, money, and love has been focused on South Street in the last five years. A renaissance of the salty past is occurring, sparked by the South Street Seaport Museum, a 15,000-member group that has so far successfully challenged the bulldozers.

The founder and president of the Seaport Museum is a former advertising man named Peter Stanford. He is quick to point out that the museum is no museum in the conventional sense: "It is not meant to be some impressive structure in which you collect a lot of artifacts of the past, but a living, functioning environment. Here we don't feel that the past is a separate attic; we believe it is something that is at the *roots* of man's experience."

Specifically, what Stanford and the museum's directors have

From *Smithsonian,* August 1971.

done is to get an eleven-block area around South Street declared an *unassisted* urban-renewal area, which means that the money for redevelopment must come from private sources. Jakob Isbrandtsen, a director of American Export Industries and chairman of the museum's board, has guaranteed a several-million-dollar loan from a consortium of six banks, and with this capital the museum has purchased the land. Member donations and seed money from a foundation have made it possible to begin refurbishing some buildings and restoring the museum's growing fleet, which at present consists of the *Ambrose* lightship, a tugboat called *Mathilda,* an old Brooklyn ferry, the schooners *Pioneer* and *Caviare,* and the enormous square-rigger *Wavertree.*

It all started in 1966, when US Attorney Whitney North Seymour Jr., a state senator in Albany at the time, introduced a bill to designate Schermerhorn Row, as the block between South and Front Streets used to be called, a maritime museum. The bill passed but without an appropriation of funds to create the museum; however, a private-sector solution to this dilemma was at hand.

Peter and Norma Stanford are weekend sailors on Long Island Sound, but they are also attracted to the waters of New York Harbor. Nautical buffs as well, they happened at the time to be looking for a disabled old schooner that could be repaired and docked there, a small but tangible reminder of the days when South Street was overshadowed by a forest of masts instead of the FDR Drive. A trip to San Francisco's Maritime Museum convinced them to enlarge their ambitions beyond schooners to square-riggers and the creation of an entire historic district of restored port-related facilities. But a seaport in someplace like Mystic, Connecticut, is one thing and a seaport on land valued at $100 a square foot is another.

Richard Buford, a city planner in the Lindsay administration, helped engineer the solution to this dilemma by working out the machinery for the transfer of air rights over the eleven blocks Isbrandtsen's consortium of banks had financed for purchase by the museum. The logic behind the transfer of air rights is this: Allow the six blocks bordering on the seaport to build higher than is otherwise permissible under the city's zoning code, while simultaneously ensuring that the five waterside blocks remain at a low five-story scale. The same amount of office space will be provided as if the whole area had been redeveloped with buildings of regularly permitted height, and the new buildings will still receive sufficient sunlight and surrounding open space since the seaport blocks act in effect as a giant plaza.

Because the museum owns the entire urban-renewal area, it will profit by the sale or lease of the transferred air rights; the city too will receive the same tax revenues it would have if the entire area had been rebuilt in the conventional fashion. In 1967, with Isbrandtsen's initial gift, $5,000, the museum took over 16 Schermerhorn Row as the first of a number of planned exhibit spaces it hopes to sprinkle throughout the South Street area.

Joseph Cantalupo, a museum board member, says, "What we've got here is better than a history book. Kids look around these streets, which are like they were when the place was a beehive of commercial and seafaring activity. I'll tell you, it means more to me for the museum to get $5.16 in contributions from the children in Grade 5 in P.S. 2 than $5,000 from Jakob Isbrandtsen. Don't get me wrong. I like everything he's doing to make the museum successful. But it's the kids caring that really counts." Cantalupo, who was himself one of the museum's earliest enthusiasts, is a son of South Street, or to be more exact, Front Street, where he and his two brothers run the rubbish-removal business they inherited from their father, Pasquale.

Cantalupo's affection for South Street is not the enthusiasm of the sailing buff ("I went out on a fishing boat twice as a kid and got sick both times"), but the enthusiasm of the city-lover. As Cantalupo explains it, this section of the city is even today as much of an ethnic bouillabaisse as were the sailing crews of old: "You have Italians, Irish, Filipinos, Eurasians, you name it." You see these people, children in tow, strolling along the museum's Pier 16, congregated around the *Caviare*, enjoying the chantey singers' free performances on Tuesday evenings in the spring and summer.

South Street is also the diurnal magnet for the office crowd that pours out of the flanking skyscrapers at noon, Monday through

Friday—the Wall Street businessmen who patronize Sweet's Restaurant and the paper-bag brigade that flocks onto Pier 16 to watch an old seadog named Ed Moran mending the rigging on the *Caviare* or just to sit on the barrels provided by the museum, with their faces upturned to catch the sunshine. Hardhats, too, from the construction sites nearby take their lunch break on the pier.

Neighborhood residents, businessmen, office workers, hardhats—all are part of the reservoir of volunteer labor that keeps the museum running. For instance, five construction men stay around South Street *donating* carpentry services to the museum after their regular working day. Printers and insurance salesmen are among the volunteers who act as information guides on Pier 16 during the busy noon hour. Every weekend, high school and college students come to Pier 16 like merchant sailors to sign on for volunteer duty. Supervising the students on Pier 16 is Doug Burris, the Seaport Museum's dockmaster and a Navy officer before he joined the Seaport staff.

Pointing to the museum's two schooners, the *Pioneer* and the *Caviare,* Burris explains, "The *Pioneer* is a Delaware River shoal-draft schooner built in 1885 to carry iron from the Chester Rolling Mills in Pennsylvania. In 1968 she was taken down to her ribs and completely reconstructed. For all intents and purposes she's a new vessel. The *Caviare* is a former Gloucester fishing schooner. Her hull is sound and she's fully rigged, but her lines are rotten in places and she's not yet seaworthy. Now, there's some controversy whether *Caviare* really was her name or not. Some people think she was the *Caviare* and others maintain she was the *Lettie G. Howard,* and when you get them arguing with each other it's like watching Civil War buffs reenacting battle scenes."

While the *Caviare* (or the *Lettie G. Howard,* as the case may be) is being renovated by volunteers, the museum's status symbol, the huge 2,100-ton *Wavertree,* is receiving professional attention under the direction of consultant William Lacey, a captain in the US Merchant Marine. According to Peter Stanford, the *Wavertree* herself has a rather ordinary story to tell; she set no records, had no famous skippers, and never flew the American flag until November 1969, when John Davis Lodge, the US ambassador to Argentina, hoisted it aboard the partly restored hulk in Buenos Aires, where the *Wavertree* had been working as a sand barge. Built in 1885, the ship had been violently dismasted off Cape Horn in 1910. Thereafter she took up an obscure life as a barge, first in Chile and then, after World War II, in Argentina. In 1968 she was presented to the South Street Seaport Museum, another gift of Jakob Isbrandtsen; a number of other citizens helped make her return possible and are engaged in raising the million dollars required for her restoration.

While the heavy, technical work of the *Wavertree* is being performed by paid labor, a lot of small jobs, such as scraping and refinishing the floors in the officers' cabins, are the work of volunteers who come to South Street expecting no remuneration for performing these dockside chores other than the opportunity to stand at the helm of the *Pioneer* as she sails on the East River into the waters of Long Island Sound.

But the Seaport is more than a place for New York Harbor recreational sailors. As Peter Stanford points out, "Nowadays yachtsmen congregate around Long Island Sound rather than Manhattan. South Street is really for those who believe in this city—both its past and its future. It is wrong to look on the volunteers opportunistically, as a way of getting the museum's work done. The museum *is* the volunteers. It exists not just *because* of them, but *for* them, so they can look at a little piece of New York and say, 'Something of my hands and head, something of *me* is here.'"

.

South Street used to be dotted with packet offices where you came to book your passage to Liverpool or Le Havre. Sailors' hotels and grog houses were salted throughout the area around Front and Pearl Streets. Also to be seen were unscrupulous runners bent on commandeering would-be inhabitants of immigrant boardinghouses as, uncertain and gullible, they stepped ashore for the first time in the United States.

Cantalupo can remember when ship chandlers were still doing business on South Street. He also recalls the tobacco warehouses, the leather-tanning establishments, printing houses, and coffee-roasting plants, the last of which moved out only last year. He says, "There was a beautiful odor to the whole place. I can't describe it to you, but it was beautiful, that combination of salt air, fish, leather, printer's ink, coffee, and tobacco."

Now only the venerable 150-year-old fish market remains, and in the next two years it is scheduled to move to new quarters in the Bronx. Although only a small group of fishermen deliver at dockside, it is still a wonderful sight to see the busy fishmongers uncrate wooden boxes of fish. Before noon the men and the trucks have cleared out, the metal bins from which the fish are sold sit empty, the fishmongers' stalls are closed down, opalescent fish scales litter the cobblestones of South Street, and an unmistakable smell lingers in the air.

The fish market will be reconstituted—a place where the lunchtime and tourist traffic can rub shoulders with the past in a relaxed fashion. It will contain seafood restaurants and oyster bars, marine-exhibit stalls, bookstores, and ship chandlers. A model shop is scheduled to open soon in an 1835 building on Water Street under the management of Martin Rockmaker, a professional miniature-ship builder.

Various house museums will be distributed throughout the five restored blocks. The Museum of American Folk Art is considering a move to Beekman and Front Streets. A museum of whaling and fisheries and a shipping museum are also being discussed. A fire museum is tentatively planned, an appropriate addition since South Street has been ravaged several times by fire in its long history.

One of the most dramatic and tragic fires occurred on the night after Christmas in 1853. The largest clipper ship in the world, the 4,555-ton *Great Republic,* was docked at the foot of Dover Street just below where the Cantalupo Carting Corporation stands today. To everyone's horror, a bakery on Front Street caught on fire, and sparks from that blaze ignited the *Great Republic*'s topsails. Firemen, half-frozen in the bitter cold, sprayed their hoses against her lower yards; the water could not reach her burning topmasts. Soon the flaming top yards came crashing onto the deck, and the conflagration roared until nothing was left of the ship but a charred hull.

But the *Great Republic* was not finished. The hull was salvaged and she was rebuilt with shortened masts and yards and three decks instead of four and remained the largest sailing ship afloat. She was used as a transport vessel for troops during the Civil War and also established a record for speed, on one occasion logging 413 miles in a single day.

Like the *Great Republic,* there is something phoenix-like about the South Street Seaport, a piece of old New York struggling to prove it is salvageable not just as a memento of the past, a curiosity for nostalgia-seekers, but as a living and necessary neighborhood within the modern city.

PART III

In and About the Parks

Green-Wood Cemetery

Scenic Repose among the Shades

(2013)

In the nineteenth century the word "sentimental" connoted nostalgia and quiet reflection; "sweet melancholy" was evoked by the fond remembrance of deceased relatives and friends. No longer was the grave a stern reminder of the transitory nature of earthly life and a warning against vanity and pride. This altered perception of death, part of the Romantic movement, stimulated the creation of the rural cemetery, in which nature's garden substituted for the urban churchyard with its rows of slab tombstones, providing an opportunity for the kind of pleasurably elegiac communion with the dead that the contemporary ethos demanded.

In a more pragmatic vein, the nineteenth century saw the rapid growth of cities. This occasioned the need for a more practical and sanitary means of interment than churchyard burial. Thus the rural cemetery, with gravesites arranged within a naturalistic park-like setting on the outskirts of the built city, became an important aspect of urban planning. Its layout incorporated the principles of the Beautiful, the Picturesque, and the Sublime, the prevailing aesthetic categories for appreciating scenery at the time. According to Romantic theory as applied to landscape design, beauty was found in the undulating green meadow, the sky-mirroring lake, and wind-

From *Green-Wood at 175: Looking Back / Looking Forward*, ed. Jeffrey Richman (Brooklyn, NY: Green-Wood Cemetery, 2013).

ing carriage roads; picturesqueness was beheld in tree-framed vistas and the rusticity of seemingly rural landscapes; and a mood of sublimity was stimulated by uplifting impressions of distant views beyond property boundaries. Embellishing raw nature with the soft, flowing lines of the beautiful, the well-placed, eye-catching effects of the picturesque, and sublime awe-inspiring glimpses of the geography of a seemingly limitless countryside became a ready-made recipe for the rural cemetery. It is not surprising therefore that these burial places would continue to attract visitors long after the Romantic movement that inspired them ran its course.

Père-Lachaise

The origins of the rural cemetery movement are found in Napoleonic France. The inspiration for a new kind of burial ground lay in the post-Revolutionary desire to found secular institutions to replace the discredited power of the Church. In 1801 legislation was passed authorizing the communes of France to purchase land outside their boundaries for public cemeteries. Two years later, the Department of the Seine created the first such cemetery on a high escarpment near the eastern edge of Paris. Known officially as the Cemetery of the East, it was called Père-Lachaise after the Jesuit priest François de La Chaise, Louis XIV's confessor, who had once owned the land. To assert the anticlerical values and nationalistic pride of Revolutionary France and confer the cachet necessary to attract purchasers of leases on surrounding burial plots, prominent resting places were assigned to such revered cultural figures as Michel de Montaigne and the legendary lovers Abelard and Heloise, and elaborate mausoleums were erected to contain their putative remains.

Laid out in a manner that combined axial geometry and monumental focal points with picturesque serpentine circuit paths and naturalistic plantings, Père-Lachaise created a new paradigm of cemetery design. A central *tapis vert* led the visitor to the site of a chapel, and on either side of this central axis were allées, which were eventually lined with impressive mausoleums built on plots held in freehold ownership by wealthy families. Nearby, at a slightly lower elevation, was an area designated as gravesites for ordinary folk. Here five-year and ten-year leaseholds served as an alternative to communal churchyard burial pits.

Americans, like the French at this time, were developing civic institutions that accorded with their republican ideals. They, too, wanted to create cemeteries that honored national history, dignified the dead, and consoled the living. In their predominantly Protestant country, however, anticlericalism was not a prominent factor, as was the case in Catholic France. Instead, Christian sentiment and belief in the resurrection of the dead furthered the ideal of family burial plots as a prelude to reunion in the hereafter, a balm for grief especially in an age when deaths of young children were commonplace. In addition, in America a strong tradition of civic leadership replaced government decree as a means of acquiring land and designing suburban cemeteries. Here, therefore, voluntary associations of citizen-reformers enlisted public support, formed corporations, and sold burial plots. Thus the rural cemetery came into being as an operation supported by private revenue rather than as a municipal institution. Its promise of perpetual rest in a beautified natural landscape meant that the cemetery corporation was responsible for its continued upkeep, an expense that was necessarily included in the cost of the individual plots.

Mount Auburn

The impulse to build rural cemeteries in America began in Boston, where patriotism was strong, voluntary associations numerous, and religion liberal. Boston was, moreover, within the intellectual orbit of Concord, where Emerson preached the philosophy of transcendentalism and extolled nature as a spiritually potent life force. The botanist, physician, and community leader Jacob Bigelow and Henry Dearborn, president of the Massachusetts Horticultural Society, were the initial advocates and creators of the first rural cemetery in America, and in 1831 they purchased a particularly beautiful, heavily wooded seventy-two-acre property in Cambridge near Harvard College, where Bigelow was a professor, for this purpose. Named Mount Auburn, it was a characteristic New England landscape of drumlins—ridges deposited by successive epochs of glaciation—with bogs and ponds left by the retreating ice. This natural scenery made it an ideal site for a Romantic design that emphasized its forested character. Over time, however, Mount Auburn acquired a different kind of beauty as its woodlands, dells, and glades, adorned with scattered burial monuments, became a series of more densely inhabited memorial gardens enriched with a mixture of exotic and native plant species.

Green-Wood

New York was not far behind Boston in creating a rural cemetery. Green-Wood, founded in 1838, provided another prototype for the burial ground as a Romantically designed naturalistic landscape. Its scenic assets were as abundant as Mount Auburn's, but instead of the forested ridges and valleys of Mount Auburn's drumlin topography, Green-Wood's landscape consisted of hills and ravines formed by the terminal moraine deposited during the last ice age by the retreating Wisconsin glacier. In addition, it boasted striking views of New York's harbor and bay, while visible in the distance were Manhattan, New Jersey, the Rockaway Peninsula, and the breakers of the Atlantic Ocean.

Henry Evelyn Pierrepont, a Brooklyn civic leader, and other prominent citizens were instrumental in the acquisition of the cemetery's original 175 acres of farmland. They formed a governing corporation to acquire subscriptions for burial plots as well as to oversee the design and maintenance of the future cemetery. One of the founding trustees, David Bates Douglass, a military and civil engineer, laid out the plan. His underlying intentions were to create "a place of repose" and not "a mere depository for dead bodies."[1] Following the aesthetic theories of William Gilpin and Uvedale Price, eighteenth-century English proponents of the picturesque style, Douglass preserved as far as possible the rustic and rural character of the landscape. Funerary architecture and sculptural features were meant to be perceived as ornamental embellishments rather than prominent focal points.

In 1839 a four-mile circuit of curvilinear roads and serpentine paths was laid out to provide access to the sites designated for monuments and family plots. Seven years later every part of the cemetery had been made accessible by broad carriage drives and winding footpaths; three thousand family lots had been sold and parts of the grounds purchased by churches and fraternal organizations. While the forested areas were kept intact for the most part, the creation of sunny glades and grass-planted lawns provided pleasantly varied vistas. The grading of topography and spreading of topsoil increased fertility, making possible the planting of flowering shrubs and trees. Relying on his knowledge of nineteenth-century technology, Douglass created a system of buried pipes to drain low-lying areas and furnish water to such features as the ponds known as Sylvan Water and Arbor Water. Later engineering augmented this infrastructure with a reservoir and water-distribution pipes.

Like Mount Auburn, Green-Wood pioneered a new kind of funerary art and architecture whose antecedents were in France where Jean-Jacques Rousseau, Romanticism's great progenitor, was buried in a neoclassical sarcophagus on a poplar-encircled island in the Marquis de Girardin's landscaped estate of Ermenonville. This alliance of nature and death, combined with classical forms borrowed from the ancient Greeks—the mausoleum, the epitaph-inscribed monument, and the funerary urn—as well as the pyramid and the obelisk derived from death-embracing ancient Egypt, provided a new memorial vocabulary based on pre-Christian antiquity. At the same time, Green-Wood was nondenominational in its character, and the style and decoration of many of its monuments were expressive of the Christian faith. In addition to kneeling angels, carved crosses, and Victorian Gothic mausoleums, the main gatehouse (1861–63) by Richard Upjohn, prominent architect of Gothic Revival churches, is a landmark example of this style. Nevertheless, the neoclassical and Egyptian designs of many other mausoleums and the numerous obelisks, urns, and columns erected as memorials to prominent individuals and revered historical personages such as DeWitt Clinton testify to another, more secular aspect of the taste of the day.

Early Green-Wood proprietors of family plots enclosed them with ornamental cast-iron-and-bronze fences or privet and boxwood hedges, and in them they erected monuments—often in anticipation of their deaths—to function as future genealogies in stone. Grass had to be kept smooth with frequent mowing, and flower beds needed regular planting and weeding. Owners were responsible for the upkeep of the individual plots, while maintenance of the overall grounds was the responsibility of the cemetery corporation. Over time, as many fences and granite curbs surrounding family plots fell into disrepair and the shrubbery defining the perimeter of others became overgrown, the trustees voted for their partial removal. In recent years, trees have been taken down in selected locations to enable visitors to regain some of the cemetery's historic views, an important example being that from Battle Hill, where the British and Americans clashed on August 26, 1776. Additional tree removal has also made it possible to see and appreciate the terraced rows of stone mausoleums and monuments ascending the slope above Sylvan Water. On the other hand, the loss of many fine specimen trees as a result of storm damage is much regretted.

Sweet Melancholy

At the time of its construction, many perceived Green-Wood Cemetery as a didactic pleasure ground, not just a domain of the departed. The cemetery's purpose as a contemplative landscape was underlined in visitors' guides with brief, inspiring biographies of the distinguished dead. In *Green-Wood Illustrated,* a lavish volume published in 1847, Nehemiah Cleaveland describes important burials in fervid prose, while James Smillie's beautiful engravings show individuals and small groups of parents, children, and friends strolling through the grounds.[2] Their attentive attitudes make it evident that visitors were intended to view Green-Wood's monuments with sentimental reflection and didactic appreciation.

The cemetery's most magnificent monument, a principal attraction for visitors, is described in another of Cleaveland's guides; it was erected by the grieving parents of Charlotte Canda, the only daughter of a wealthy French émigré, following her death in 1845. Cleaveland's paean extolling the virtues and accomplishments of the seventeen-year-old girl is lavish, and his narrative of the carriage accident in which she met her end is filled with tender pathos. Her marble Gothic mausoleum, with its profusion of tracery surrounding a niche with a pointed arch, is buttressed by delicately carved, seventeen-foot-tall twin spires. Her age, denoted by the height of the spires, is also alluded to by the floral finials composed of seventeen bunched roses crowning the monument's miniature gables. Seventeen rosebuds intertwined with ivy and encircled by seventeen stars are carved on each of the lower panels. Escutcheons bearing her monogram of intertwined Cs adorn the side panels along with birds, ivy garlands, fleurs-de-lis, and more flowers.[3]

In addition to fostering elegiac emotion, Cleaveland was fond of adding moral interpretations to his descriptions of monuments. These remarks were intended to inspire viewers to reflect on the importance of virtue, duty, patriotism, and the benefit to others of leading an exemplary life. For example, although Battle Hill marks a humiliating American defeat and Washington's evacuation of his forces on Long Island, Cleaveland tells his readers that "these and more, —the reluctant abandonment of the city, —the cowardice and desertion of the militia, —the loss of the forts, —and that sad retreat of the reduced, discouraged, barefooted, and half-naked army through the Jerseys, —were all needed. . . . Without these we had not fully known how inherent, how enduring and elastic is the power of an earnest and virtuous patriotism."[4]

In a similar vein, Cleaveland sermonizes on the meaning of Pilot's Monument. Visible from the harbor like a beacon, this memorial— a sarcophagus surmounted by a marble mast—commemorates Thomas Freeborn, who was drowned as he tried to bring the ship *John Minturn* into New York Harbor during a severe storm on

February 14, 1846. Its truncated top is crowned by a small statue of Hope supported by an anchor. This conspicuous object, Cleaveland writes, "will often arrest the eye of the pilot as he goes and comes on his hazardous but responsible errands. If it remind him of his own possible fate, —it will assure him also that the faithful discharge of duty is never without its encouragement."[5]

Cleaveland sometimes interpolates his eulogies with fanciful storytelling. In the case of the monument on Indian Mound, he engages his reader with a pathetic tale of Do-hom-me, a beautiful eighteen-year-old Sac maiden who had journeyed from the Far West to Washington, DC, where her chieftain father had traveled to negotiate a land dispute. Along the way Do-hom-me fell in love with an Iowa warrior who was a member of their traveling party. The two were duly married according to tribal rites and began their union in a state of bliss. Curious to see other great cities of the Atlantic seaboard, they came to New York, where Do-hom-me fell ill and died. Cleaveland invites us to imagine how "the helpless bewilderment—the agony, almost despair, of the doting father and husband—their piteous wails and sobs—the irrepressible tears which, unwiped, flowed down their dusky cheeks, altogether formed a picture which can never be forgotten and which forever disproves the oft-told tale of the Indian's coldness and stoicism." Sounding the prevalent theme of family reunion after death, he describes her burial "in a spot aptly chosen for the grave of the forest-girl, [where] she reposes in the last, dreamless slumber." Embosomed in Green-Wood's beautiful landscape, "she hears not the ocean-winds that sigh around her green-roofed dwelling; the footsteps of the frequent pilgrim disturb her not;—for, let us believe that, according to her own simple faith, her spirit is lovingly, patiently waiting, in some far-off but happy sphere, till those she so loved on earth shall join her, never more to be separated."[6]

Storied monuments like these account for the immediate popularity of Green-Wood as a place for a quiet outing. More than this, however, was the salubrious and scenic nature of the site as a place of escape from the busy city. While it had been created as a Brooklyn institution, Green-Wood was easily accessible by ferry from Manhattan, and it quickly became a place of popular resort for the residents of New York City and numerous tourists as well. On Sundays ferries crossed the bay carrying holidaymakers whose intentions were simply to enjoy an outing rather than to mourn the dead or be uplifted by the meanings of monuments. By 1860 an estimated five hundred thousand visitors flocked there annually.

Because of its recreational popularity, Green-Wood became the prototype for another kind of Romantic landscape. In the July 1849 issue of his magazine, *The Horticulturist,* Andrew Jackson Downing, the influential Hudson River Valley landscape designer, pointed out that "the great attraction of these cemeteries, to the mass of the community, is not in the fact that they are burial-places, or solemn places of meditation for the friends of the deceased, or striking exhibitions of monumental sculpture, though all these have their influence." Rather, he maintained, "The true secret of the attraction lies in the natural beauty of the sites, and in the tasteful and harmonious embellishment of these by art." "Does not this general interest," he queried rhetorically, "prove that public gardens, established in a liberal and suitable manner, near our large cities, would be equally successful?" It was a logical next step to envision a democratic people's park in which associations with death, however poetical these might be, were absent. Not surprisingly, in the August 1851 issue of *The Horticulturist* Downing published a hortatory article titled "The New-York Park" in which he laid out a compelling case for the creation of what would soon become Central Park.[7]

As parks took on some of the recreational purposes once associated with rural cemeteries, the significance of the latter shifted and Green-Wood gained lasting fame as a memorial ground for Civil War generals, legendary baseball players, politicians, artists, musicians, actors, inventors, and other celebrities. Included on its Who's Who list are such notables as Leonard Bernstein, Boss Tweed, Charles Ebbets, Jean-Michel Basquiat, Louis Comfort Tiffany, and Horace Greeley.

Green-Wood's continued popularity as a burial site resulted in the acquisition of contiguous parcels of land over the years; its present size is 478 acres. As a growing number of plots were sold, the cemetery's shady groves adorned with isolated monuments were transformed into a more horticultural type of landscape. At the same time, the site retained much of its original arboreal splendor, and today numerous trees that were planted a century ago have attained majestic proportions. Notable among the landscape's botanical treasures are European beeches, oaks, lindens, sweet gums, horse chestnuts, maples, Douglas firs, London plane trees, cucumber magnolias, ginkgos, katsuras, hickories, Turkish filberts, persimmons, Himalayan pines, and tulip poplars.

For botanical enthusiasts the arboretum character of Green-Wood is a prime attraction. In addition, its dense tree canopy makes it a green urban oasis for birdlife. Hosting over two hundred avian species, the cemetery is now a registered member of the Audubon Cooperative Sanctuary System. Lying within the Atlantic Flyway, during the spring and fall it is an important stopover for migratory songbirds, including wood warblers, vireos, tanagers, wrens, cedar waxwings, indigo buntings, and many others. Its ponds attract several kinds of waterbirds, among them herons, egrets, geese, ducks, grebes, cormorants, and kingfishers. Vultures and bald eagles have been spotted overhead, and ruby-throated hummingbirds, juncos, pipits, thrashers, owls, and Eastern bluebirds are regularly spotted by keen-eyed bird-watchers. Year-round residents include red-tailed hawks, cardinals, blue jays, nuthatches, titmice, rock pigeons, starlings, and—most improbably—a colony of escaped monk parakeets that breed year after year in the high arches of Upjohn's magnificent entrance gate.

•

No historic landscape remains static, and Green-Wood's will continue to alter over time. Because of the cemetery's continued popularity and the high level of stewardship it now enjoys, its future as one of the city's greatest green places is promising. Indeed, its founders would rejoice in the fact that, 175 years after they laid it out, this early rural cemetery's Romantic roots are still mostly intact and it remains a place of peaceful pleasure for the 250,000 living souls who join its 560,000 permanent residents in experiencing tranquility and repose amid scenes of nature, art, and history each year.

Designing Prospect Park

(2016)

In 1859, when Frederick Law Olmsted was overseeing the initial stages of Central Park's construction, Brooklyn made its bid for a similarly large pleasure ground. A bill authorizing a park was passed by the state legislature that year, but the Civil War prevented the Brooklyn park commissioners from carrying out work other than designating boundaries and awarding compensation for the park's original 350 acres straddling Flatbush Avenue.

In 1861 Central Park's former engineer, Egbert Viele, submitted a drawing labeled "A Plan for the Improvement of Prospect Park." This name was derived from Mount Prospect, the high hill at the intersection of Flatbush Avenue and what later became Eastern Parkway. The park that Viele envisioned consisted of two lozenge-shaped parcels connected by overpasses across Flatbush Avenue. But although he was sanguine about the bisected park plan, some of the commissioners apparently were not. Calvert Vaux was called in to survey the park grounds and make suggestions for redefining its boundaries. Immediately struck by the awkwardness of the proposed site, he suggested that the eastern portion of the park be sold off and the proceeds used to acquire additional land to the west. More than a mere increase in acreage, the annexed land

Unpublished essay. The first section is based on the chapter on Prospect Park in my book *Frederick Law Olmsted's New York* (New York: Praeger, 1972).

would expand the park visitor's illusion of space by making possible long, sweeping vistas. Vaux drew up an initial report on boundaries, to which he appended a diagram of a reconfigured site showing a rough disposition of the park into three main elements: lake, rugged woodland, and an extensive rolling meadow. Refined, this sketch plan became the basic blueprint for Prospect Park.

Olmsted had been the head of the Sanitary Commission, the forerunner of the Red Cross, during the Civil War, a job he performed between 1861 and 1863. Then, with no particular desire to return to New York and recommence his career as a landscape designer, he accepted an offer to be the resident manager of a mining operation in California. Vaux, however, did not to wish to proceed independently as sole designer of Prospect Park, and he therefore wanted to renew the partnership that had resulted in the creation of Central Park. He wrote Olmsted repeatedly, urging him to return to New York. Recalling their collaboration on Central Park, he said:

> If . . . you had been disheartened—there very likely might have been no park to chatter about today, for I alone was wholly incompetent to take it up. . . . I had no idea of competing because I felt my incapacity. I feel it no less—I will not say no less, but very little less—now, and enter on Brooklyn alone with hesitation and distrust not on the roads and walks or even planting . . . but in regard to the main point—the translation of the republican art idea in its highest form into the acres we want to control.[1]

A few months earlier Olmsted had written:

> I can't tell you, I say again, how attractive to me the essential business we had together is; nor how I abhor the squabbles with the Commission and politicians. Both are very deep with me. I feel them deeper every year. It was a passion thwarted and my whole life is really embittered with it very much. . . . I think a good deal how I should I like to show you what I really am and could do with a perfectly free and fair under-

standing from the start, and with a moderate degree of freedom from the necessity of accommodating myself to infernal
scoundrels. I have a perfect craving for the park, sometimes,
and for an exposition from you of what I want.

But, bother!

Your plans are excellent, of course, you don't play with it
but go at once to the essential starting points, and I hope the
Commissioners are wise enough to comprehend it. I think
the ground looks attractive, as if you could form a much simpler and grander and more convenient kind of Park than ours
on it.[2]

Even though his association with Mariposa Mines was drawing
to a close, Olmsted, who in 1859 had married his brother John's
widow, Mary, thought he would stay on in California to nurture
other investments that would leave his family financially secure
should he die. Vaux continued to urge him to return to New York,
saying, "There is a nauseous sort of flavor about Park matters to me
that it will be difficult to get over on this side of the grave. However
never say die. . . . We may have some fun together yet. I wish you
could have seen your destiny in our art. God meant you should. I
really believe at times, although he may have something different
for you to do, yet he cannot have anything nobler in store for you."[3]

Olmsted was reluctant to confuse avocation with aptitude. Curiously, he still considered himself a dabbler in landscape art:

I am sorry to say that I do not feel myself capable of being a
landscape gardener, —properly speaking—but I have a better and more cultivated taste in that department of art than
any other, very much—having none in any other—and if I
had the necessary quality of memory, or if my memory had
been educated in botany and gardening when I was young,
I might have been. But I can do anything with proper assis-
tants, or money enough—anything that any man can do. I
can combine means to ends better than most, and I love beautiful landscapes and rural recreations and people in rural rec-

reations—better than anybody else I know. But I don't feel strong on the art side. I don't feel myself an artist, I feel rather as if it was sacrilegious in me to post myself in the portals of Art. . . .

I have none of your feeling of nauseousness about the park. There is no other place in the world that is as much home to me. I love it all through and all the more for the trials it has cost me.

I should like very well to go into the Brooklyn Park, or anything else—if I really believed I could get a decent living out of it—but in landscape work in general I never had any ground for supposing that I could. You used to argue that I might hope to—that's all. I could never see it.[4]

But, overcoming his own objections at last, Olmsted agreed to return to New York and partner with Vaux once more, a decision that determined not only his own future but also the birth of the profession of landscape architecture in America.

.

Facilitating the design of Prospect Park was the boundary revision that eliminated the originally planned bisection of the proposed site by Flatbush Avenue. At Vaux's suggestion, the Brooklyn commissioners agreed to exchange land acquired to the east for contiguous farmland to the south, thereby gaining a much better-shaped site. Now the park's design would not be constrained by a preexisting street plan such as the one that had resulted in the long and narrow rectangular configuration of Central Park. In addition, Prospect Park's topography was inherently more suitable for park purposes. Situated on the terminal moraine deposited in the wake of the last period of North American glaciation, its natural landscape was already a gently undulating one with decent topsoil unlike that of the Manhattan park whose topsoil had to be imported and ground plane extensively regraded in order to provide an agreeably varied topography and the necessary depth of soil for planting. Moreover, with altering the original boundaries the park gained a low-lying area well suited for the creation of an artificial lake larger than the one in Central Park. There was a final advantage as well: the original acres reserved for the park on the eastern side of Flatbush Avenue could now be allocated to the construction of both a museum and a botanical garden.

Adhering to Vaux's original tripartite scheme of meadow, woods, and water, the collaborators arranged their views and vistas of pastoral and sylvan scenery. Conceiving recreation to be primarily a visual experience, they laid out pathways and carriage drives as a series of vantage points for enjoying the park's carefully arranged landscape compositions. In a brilliant move on their part to give the impression that the park had no defined boundaries with vistas checked by a wall of buildings, the Long Meadow was designed as a rolling greensward with little hillocks fringed by woods concealing the surrounding urban neighborhood.

In the report accompanying their plan, Olmsted and Vaux were quite specific about what constituted their simulation of pastoral scenery. "It consists of combinations of trees, standing singly or in groups, and casting their shadows over broad stretches of turf, or repeating their beauty by reflection upon the calm surface of pools, . . . stony ravines shaded with trees, and made picturesque with shrubs, [and] some slight approach to the mystery, variety and luxuriance of tropical scenery, . . . gay with flowers, and intricate and mazy with vines and creepers, ferns, rushes and broadleaved plants."[5]

The forest groves between the Long Meadow and the Nethermead are the picturesque-style counterpart of Central Park's Ramble. A little stream, with a series of pools created by water pumped from the lake, meanders like a mountain brook through these woods. On an island in the lake, lush plantings provided an illusion of tropical vegetation. The designers realized, however, that people visit parks not only to admire nature but also to socialize with one another. They observed, "Men must come together, and must be seen coming together, in carriages, on horseback and on foot, and the concourse of animated life which will thus be formed, must in itself be made, if possible, an attractive and diverting spectacle."[6]

As on the Central Park Mall, there would be a concert ground for gatherings of people from all classes of society, which in the case of Prospect Park took the form of a pedestrian concourse flanked by rows of tree-shaded seats facing a music stand sited on an island in the bay of the lake.

Taking the circuit of Central Park's drives in one's landau or brougham had become an established social rite with people of fashion. A similar parade of Brooklyn notables would be accommodated by an oval carriage concourse on Vanderbilt Hill crowned by the Lookout, a viewing tower that was never built, although the unadorned hillcrest is still a cool and pleasant eminence for a bird's-eye view of the park and its now-urbanized environs. The Refectory, a planned but never realized counterpart to the Casino café in Central Park, was designed like a country inn and situated on the lakeshore in a location where it could serve skaters in winter and boating parties in summer. In such ways as these Prospect Park, like Central Park, was planned to satisfy two contrasting objectives—the desire for tranquility and solitude and the wish for animated spectacle and gregariousness.

The 1866 report to the Brooklyn park commissioners extended the designers' purview beyond the boundaries of Prospect Park and showed evidence of Olmsted's growing concern with matters of urban planning. Already recognizing the demand to use Central Park as a site for locating various institutional structures, Olmsted and Vaux wished to obviate similar encroachments in Prospect Park. They were helped by the fact that the land that had been previously acquired but then discarded for park purposes on the east side of Flatbush Avenue was now available for other uses. Thus, unlike the Metropolitan Museum, which was imposed on Central Park, the Brooklyn Museum would have an independent site of its own. Since a surrounding street grid was yet to be platted, the designers were not constrained from suggesting the remapping of the thoroughfares facing the principal entrance in order that they might terminate at its double-crescent plaza at a better angle.

More important than the reconfiguration of the street pattern adjacent to the park was the proposal labeled "Suburban Connections." Though the word "parkway" would not be coined until Olmsted and Vaux submitted their 1868 report to the park's board of commissioners, the concept was embodied two years earlier in the 1866 report. "Such a road," they stated, "whatever may be the character of the country through which it passes, should be in itself of a picturesque character. It should, therefore, be neither very straight nor very level, and should be bordered by a small belt of trees and shrubbery."[7] Specifically, they had in mind a pleasure drive connecting the park with the sea. Ocean Parkway, when built, was straight, not curvilinear, but its functional separation of traffic by tree-planted malls into carriageway, walks, and access roads is an important innovation in the history of American road building.

If a single road for pleasure driving was good, even better would be an entire system of scenic roads. Anticipating the Queensboro Bridge, Olmsted and Vaux envisioned another parkway starting from Prospect Park and carried over the East River to connect with Central Park. They hoped that north of Central Park the future development of Manhattan would incorporate an additional system of scenic roads to take the pleasure driver within sight of the Hudson River and the Palisades in New Jersey.

·

Following its submission, the plan for Prospect Park was circulated among the citizens of Brooklyn. With far less division of opinion than had been the case with Central Park, it was declared acceptable, and an application to the state legislature to authorize the proposed boundary change was made. On May 29, 1866, Olmsted and Vaux were formally appointed landscape architects for the park. Cart gangs and barrow gangs were hired, and the labor of grading, filling, and draining was begun. Fourteen thousand trees were set out as initial stock in two nurseries on the park premises.

In their report of the following year, the landscape architects articulated once again the parkway concept. This time they proposed laying out such a road in anticipation of the development that would take place to the east of Prospect Park. They believed that a spacious and agreeable thoroughfare would attract the settlement of families desiring suburban villas. When built, Eastern Parkway was straight, in the manner of a French boulevard, rather than picturesque with "frequent curves and considerable inequalities of surface" as Olmsted and Vaux had suggested.[8] Its real significance was as a demonstration of the relationship between transportation and urban development.

A landmark document in the history of city planning, the 1868 report is a brief for the differentiation of various classes of roads according to their intended function and adjacent land use. It includes a review of the nature and condition of roads from feudal times to the nineteenth century, from the random footpaths of the medieval town to the grid plan of the urban land speculator. It points out how London merchants, ignoring Christopher Wren's sensible street widening and straightening proposal following the Great Fire of 1666, rebuilt their city on old property lines rather than in a logical form that would serve the common interest. The result was the delay for a century of a pattern of straight connected streets with raised sidewalks for pedestrians and gutters underlain by sewers for carrying away refuse. According to the report, now that cities were no longer compact defense fortresses, with houses and workshops occupying the same structures and the whole urban mass tightly packed behind walls, a great amelioration of the human condition had occurred. There was a lower rate of disease and pestilence, fewer fires, and less vandalism and mob violence.[9]

Clairvoyantly, Olmsted and Vaux predicted the phenomenal urban growth of the twentieth century; they foresaw the spread of the city over a continually increasing land base. Devoted as they were to the aesthetic of the pastoral and picturesque, they nevertheless saw the futility of trying to turn the clock back to an earlier, simpler America. They grasped the implications of the new technology that was being developed in the years immediately after the Civil War: the laying of the transatlantic cable, the construction of the railroad to the Pacific, the opening of Europe and the Far East to steam navigation. These and other innovations in transportation and communications would, they predicted, greatly stimulate trade, thereby making the enlargement of cities inevitable. The same technology that brought people together in cities also made it possible for them to spread out and live in relative seclusion from one another. The suburb with its leafy gardens was the product of the commuter railroad and the macadam highway.

The suburban ideal, discredited in our own time because its full-scale realization has resulted in diffuse, un-centered, sprawling urbanization, was actually an important nineteenth-century contribution to the art of city building. At that time the suburb promised pure air and sunlight and the oxygen-generating capacity of green plants surrounding each domicile. Olmsted firmly believed that the detached villa was a far healthier residence than the row house, the basic middle-class dwelling type of that day, and he never ceased campaigning for the subdivision of land into lots one hundred or more feet in width. The suburb, like the park, served a psychophysical purpose. It was a good compromise in the instinctive longing for verdure, which most people, especially those who had once lived amid rural surroundings, felt in the engulfing city.

Further, Olmsted and Vaux believed that, although a grid street plan was advantageous in the commercial sector where the direct movement of goods was desirable, it was incompatible with the character of a suburb. The popularity of driving as a form of recreation dictated the need for smooth roadbeds and pleasant, tree-shaded thoroughfares, preferably curvilinear, connecting parks with residential neighborhoods. To prohibit commercial traffic on such roads would be impossible inasmuch as the homes adjoining them would have to be serviced by vehicles of trade. Thus, as a logical refinement in the history of road building to meet the needs of the nineteenth-century city, the Prospect Park designers offered the parkway with its central drive, flanking promenades, exterior access roads, and sidewalks, all separated by rows of trees. They reasoned, moreover, that the width of this multipurpose thoroughfare made it a perfect fire barrier. In addition, the parkway system emanating from Prospect Park was the frame upon which at least a part of residential Brooklyn would grow. By extending the boundaries of their plan beyond those specified in their original design commission and thereby causing them to encompass the entire undeveloped section of Brooklyn, Olmsted and Vaux articulated the importance of intelligent, comprehensive city planning in advance of future urban growth at a time when that kind of foresight was practically unknown.

Continuing their professional association, in 1868 following the completion of the design of their comprehensive plan for Prospect Park, Olmsted and Vaux implemented their urban planning principles in Buffalo, New York, where they laid out an entire park system linked by parkways. In 1873, following this success, the two men dissolved their partnership, and ten years later Olmsted moved to Brookline, Massachusetts, where he established an independent landscape design practice. There he worked in affiliation with the architect Henry Hobson Richardson on the creation of Boston's Emerald Necklace, another system of interconnected parks and parkways, while Vaux remained in New York where he formed a partnership with the landscape architect Samuel Parsons Jr.

Altering Prospect Park

Because it never held the same kind of attraction for various building schemes and memorials, Prospect Park retained more of its original design intentions than its Manhattan predecessor and remains perhaps the best paradigm of an Olmstedian park today. Like Central Park, however, in the 1890s it received the attentions of a new generation of architects schooled in the principles of Beaux-Arts neoclassicism—a style antithetical to the picturesque design principles espoused by Olmsted and Vaux.[10]

An independent city until 1898, Brooklyn rivaled New York City in its aspirations to metropolitan grandeur. The City Beautiful movement which flourished during the 1890s and on through the 1920s constituted America's industrial-age urban aggrandizement in the manner of Napoleon III's nineteenth-century Paris. Chicago's "White City," Daniel Burnham's plan for the Columbian Exposition of 1893, was the American paradigm. Although Olmsted was the principal landscape designer of the fairgrounds, it was the École des

Beaux-Arts–trained members of the team who inherited Burnham's neoclassical mantle. These included the architects Richard Morris Hunt and the firm of Charles McKim, William Mead, and Stanford White and the sculptors Augustus Saint-Gaudens, Frederick Mac-Monnies, and Daniel Chester French. In the years to follow these men often received collaborative commissions that set the style for urban embellishment with monumental public works of art.

At Grand Army Plaza, Prospect Park's principal entrance, McKim, Mead & White reconfigured Olmsted and Vaux's original elliptical plaza with a two-section, curving granite colonnade and Ionic columns, and MacMonnies was responsible for the sculpture ornamenting John H. Duncan's Soldiers' and Sailors' Monument, a triumphal arch with a crowning quadriga recalling the one atop Saint Mark's Basilica in Venice. Other monumental entrances superseded the rustic pavilions and rows of trees preferred by Olmsted and Vaux, including a neoclassical peristyle below the South Lake Drive and across from the east end of the Parade Ground, which in turn was replaced by three even larger neoclassical structures by the firm of Helmle, Huberty & Hudswell. The same firm's debut structure in the park is the current Boathouse, which replaced the original wooden one on the east side of the long arm of the Lake known as the Lullwater. Built in 1905, its design was borrowed from the lower story of Jacopo Sansovino's Marciana Library in Venice. Helmle, Huberty & Hudswell were subsequently hired to design the Tennis House, which was constructed in 1909–10 as an open loggia on the west side of the Long Meadow. At 9th Street and Prospect Park West stands the monument honoring the Marquis de Lafayette, a bronze sculptural plaque in high relief by Daniel Chester French, which is set within a neoclassical pink granite frame designed by Henry Bacon.

Brooklyn's amalgamation into the City of Greater New York in 1898 ushered in its eclipse as a proud independent municipality, and World War I spelled an end to its competitive impulse toward civic grandeur. With the exception of the Honor Roll Memorial, with bronze tablets inscribed with the names of Brooklyn soldiers killed in the war and a central sculpture of a wounded soldier with a hovering Angel of Death ready to embrace him, which was placed next to the Lake to the east of Music Island, Prospect Park's era of neoclassicism was at an end. Only a single remaining echo of this style is found in the Palladian entry arch of the 1927 red-brick Picnic House overlooking the Long Meadow.

In spite of these encroachments—several of which are now admired as Beaux-Arts masterpieces—Olmsted and Vaux's overall landscape vision for Prospect Park did not especially suffer until Robert Moses arrived on the scene. With the same characteristic disregard for the historic design he displayed in Central Park during his tenure as mid-twentieth-century commissioner of the city's parks department, Moses inserted hardscape recreational facilities into Prospect Park and tore down some of the picturesque structures that Olmsted and Vaux had woven into the fabric of the landscape. The same sort of redbrick buildings with limestone trim that appeared in Central Park were also constructed in Prospect Park as replacements for the rustic wooden structures favored by the original designers. These included the animal houses of the zoo, designed by Moses's favorite architect, Aymar Embury II, who was also responsible for the 1939 design of the Bandshell, located off Prospect Park West between 10th and 11th Streets. As in Central Park, Moses had the former carousel replaced with a historic Coney Island carousel housed in an octagonal structure of banded yellow and red brick.

There was worse to come in terms of the destruction of Olmsted and Vaux's design intentions when, in 1959, a fenced-in complex of seven ball fields with bleachers was constructed at the north end of the Long Meadow. A year later this was followed by the desecration of the Concert Grove and obliteration of Music Stand Island by a 140-by-200-foot ice-skating rink surrounded by a high metal fence. As was the case with the rinks Moses built at the Harlem Meer and Pond in Central Park, this one was constructed over a particularly beautiful cove of the Lake.

Again, as in the case of Central Park, what followed the Moses regime was management neglect, crime associated with the drug culture, and rampant vandalism. Here also lawns and meadows turned into hardpan, the Ravine and Lake became silted, and since the park's water system is self-contained, its sluggish flow compounded the problem of eutrophication. Destruction of ornamental stonework, broken lights, graffiti, unpruned trees, and weedy undergrowth signaled the park's dereliction. Fortunately, however, as in Central Park, the fortunes of Prospect Park were reversed in 1980 when a new era of restoration and improved management begun.

Renewing Prospect Park

The appointment of Tupper Thomas as Prospect Park administrator by Mayor Edward I. Koch marked the beginning of a thirty-year turnaround in the way the park is cared for and perceived by the public. Thomas, who was the administrator and founding president of the Prospect Park Alliance, a public–private partnership modeled on the Central Park Conservancy, has much to be proud of. Her successes have been due in large measure to her genial personality and ability to entice the surrounding community to once again assume a sense of ownership of the park. With some private philanthropic support, though considerably less than that which buoyed the fortunes of Central Park, she worked with Brooklyn's elected officials and parks department staff members to channel city dollars into the park for badly needed capital projects. Her good management oversight and a small but exceedingly loyal staff and a dedicated contingent of volunteers helped maintain the park as, piece by piece, its ongoing landscape restoration and the historic preservation of its Beaux-Arts structures have been accomplished and its Moses-era facilities integrated more sympathetically into its nineteenth-century landscape heritage.

A recent desire to see Prospect Park's ongoing reincarnation prompted me to schedule a tour with Tupper, a close friend because of the common park renewal experiences she and I were engaged in simultaneously during the time I was the administrator of Central Park. After we rendezvoused on a beautiful early June day at the entrance next to Daniel Chester French's monument to General Lafayette, we walked into the north end of the park and stood beside the complex of ball fields that many historic landscape preservationists still deplore as an abomination and insult to the quintessence of Olmstedian scenery: the Long Meadow with its illusionistic impression of rural infinity. As was the case in Central Park, it would have been political suicide to remove the Moses ball fields and restore the site to greensward, and it was here that early in her administration Thomas's skill as a friendly negotiator became evident.

"I met with John Cortese," she told me. "He was the head of the Umpires, an association of ball field permit holders, which came into existence as a way of working out the fighting between the various teams competing for playing time. I told him we wanted to tear down the tall chain-link fence and make the ball fields more scenically integrated with the rest of the Long Meadow. At the time, people thought the fence was a necessity for safety reasons, but I was able to get John to come around. He actually said, 'This park is the most beautiful place in the world. I have been coming here all my life, so I understand what you are trying to do.' That was it, since he had control over the various teams and could reason with each of them."

We stopped near the western edge of the Long Meadow to look at the restored Tennis House, beneath whose grand Italianate loggia the park's maintenance workers now have their headquarters, along with the staff that runs educational programs. "When it was first constructed, tennis players had their lockers above and would keep their nets and other equipment in the space down below. Spectators could sit beneath those big arches and watch the players. There were no level clay courts, of course; people just came out and had games on the lawn just as it was. Unfortunately, after we restored the Tennis House there was still so much graffiti going on in the park that we had to put up this tall fence. It was a mistake back then to restore buildings without being able to staff them properly, but still it made people understand that the historic park mattered. Maybe someday we'll be able to take the fence down and have a real public use for the building."

After we had admired the soft, pinkish terra-cotta of the restored Guastavino tiles cladding the underside of the arches' vaulting, we walked further into the Long Meadow, where scattered clumps of trees accent and define the green sweep of the expansive landscape. Picnickers and romping schoolchildren dotted the scene. "You don't have to tell people," Tupper said. "They get it. An Olmsted landscape speaks for itself. It's plain gorgeous!"

Because of our parallel career paths, it was natural that we would talk shop. "You had archival documents to work from," Tupper said. "We had nothing. All the Olmsted and Vaux plans and working drawings and planting plans had either been destroyed or someone had stolen them. We've looked and looked and can't find anything, even historical photos. There are only a few scattered notes that we've ever come across." Pointing to a stand of magnificent elms, she said, "We don't know if this is exactly what was planted in this location, but they are certainly in the spirit of what was intended to be planted on top of some of the knolls like this one."

"It's an entirely different kind of landscape," she continued. "Because this part of Brooklyn is a product of the last glacier's terminal moraine, in Prospect Park Olmsted and Vaux didn't have bedrock outcrops protruding everywhere as they did in Central Park. Here there were already rolling hills, valleys, and dells, with lots of sand and boulders beneath the surface. They were so brilliant in the way they used these." We had passed a small pond protected by a fence except for an opening where there is a small beach made of what she called "sandcrete" and a scrap of enclosed water in which dogs can paddle and children swim. Demonstrating once more the value of diplomatic community relations in reforming public behavior, Tupper said, "If we opened the whole perimeter of the pond it would be trampled the way it was before, and there would be no vegetation left, so we made a compromise with just a little bit of controlled access to the water. If you look around the shoreline now you can see how beautiful and lush the vegetation is. People, especially the bird-watchers, like it a lot."

We next paused at the head of the Ravine in front of the tall waterfall that tumbles over a mass of boulders. "This," Tupper explained, "is the single source of all the water throughout the park. You see, in Brooklyn at the time the park was built they didn't have any sewers, so the entire system had to be one continuous piece of circulating water. From this point it feeds the Upper Pond and Lower Pond where we just were; then it flows into the stream running through the Ravine into the Lullwater; from there it goes into the Lake itself. It was a fantastic piece of hydrological engineering!"

Tupper is a welcome presence whenever she returns to Prospect Park. Now, as I was admiring the cascading water tumbling over the mass of boulders that had been repositioned during the Ravine's extensive recent renovation, she cried out, "Oh, Christian, it's you! I was just telling Betsy about how all the rocks had fallen down and how you picked out each one and supervised how they were set in place." Christian Zimmerman, who has worked in Prospect Park during Tupper's tenure and beyond, had been her right-hand employee. He is a horticulturist as well as a landscape architect, and his knowledge of both plant material and landscape design continues to be critical to the success of Prospect Park's ongoing restoration.

Like Central Park, Prospect Park is a landscape masterpiece—maybe even the greatest masterpiece—of Olmsted and Vaux's design collaboration. It was obvious from the tour I had just taken with Tupper that the same combination of art and nature that had been their uppermost intention was being ingeniously reestablished here through an ongoing partnership of restoration planners and on-site managers working together on a day-to-day basis.

Robert Moses and the
Transformation of Central Park

(2007)

For the past thirty-five years, landscape historians have been reviving the reputation of Frederick Law Olmsted, the design partner with Calvert Vaux of the Greensward plan for Central Park and the founder of the landscape architecture profession in America. During twenty-five years of this time the park itself has enjoyed a period of restoration and good management through the coordinated efforts of New York City's parks department and the Central Park Conservancy.

This renaissance is but the latest chapter in the park's checkered 150-year history. Central Park was conceived as a place where city dwellers could promenade on foot or parade in carriages, enjoying the artfully conceived scenery and social spectacle. But by the early twentieth century the concept of scenic recreation—movement through a visual sequence of lawns, woods, and bodies of water—was no longer considered the park's paramount purpose. Samuel Parsons Jr., who followed Vaux as the parks department's head landscape architect from 1898 until 1911, presided over the end of what may be called the park's Greensward era, the period when it was managed according to the vision of Olmsted and Vaux. Subsequently, social reformers of the Progressive Era believed that people needed more than simple contact with naturalistic scenery,

From *Site/Lines* 3.1 (Fall 2007).

and parks commissioners began to view Central Park in a different light, as a place to play games. The profession of recreation leader was born, and a cadre of city employees was hired to organize sports activities in parks throughout the city in an effort to improve the health of slum children and help them move into the American cultural mainstream.

·

Although Olmsted oversaw the general plan and designed the naturalistic lake with its picturesque Wooded Island for the 1893 Columbian Exhibition in Chicago, it was Daniel Burnham's monumental vision for the fair's buildings, as well as for the city of Chicago itself, that influenced a new generation of architects, thereby launching the City Beautiful movement in American urban design. Its neoclassical legacy in Central Park is due in part to two newspaper moguls, William Randolph Hearst and Joseph Pulitzer. The antithesis of Vaux's picturesque-style architecture, Hearst's grandiose 1913 USS *Maine* Monument rises above the southwest entrance of Central Park, and the 1916 Pulitzer Fountain ornaments Grand Army Plaza at the southeast corner.

Central Park, however, changed little in its overall appearance during that time except for the wear and tear it received from hosting an increasing number of celebrations and group activities. The onslaught of automobile traffic by the 1920s transformed its pastoral character more completely. While the park's naturalistic landscape had its defenders, increasingly it came to be seen as a site for monuments and other encroachments. Several bizarre proposals were put forth, including a landing field for aircraft, a track for horse races, a central fire station, a burial ground for war heroes, an opera house, and a series of trenches commemorating the 1916 Battle of Verdun. These multiple unrelated proposals were symptomatic of government and citizen leadership's failure to understand either the park's scenic or recreational purposes. In 1934 this state of affairs came to a decisive halt. Henceforth one man would conceive, execute, and publicize every alteration of its landscape for the next twenty-six years. That man was Robert Moses.

Moses's vision of public service grew out of the reform movement of the Progressive Era. When he was appointed by Mayor Fiorello La Guardia as parks commissioner in 1934, Moses assumed the necessary power to give permanent form to his early twentieth-century predecessors' previous efforts to make Central Park a place for active recreation. Instead of allowing sports to take place by simply abandoning the old regulations as they had done, however, he dedicated portions of the park to specific activities: lawns became bowling and croquet greens, and meadows were turned into ball fields. And discontinuing the tradition of skating on the natural ice of Central Park's Pond, Lake, and Harlem Meer, he built two permanent ice-skating rinks.

At the time Moses came to office, the only playground in the park was one created in 1926 near Seventh Avenue and 63rd Street, a gift from the philanthropist August Heckscher. In September 1935, nineteen fenced-off playgrounds with large sandboxes—"places where children can dig" as Moses characterized these then-novel features—were opened near park entrances. In October of the following year, three more playgrounds were added. Enthusiastically adopted by mothers and children, they were touted by Moses as a way to preserve the surrounding scenery. To further discourage romping on the grass, he encircled lawns with pipe rail fencing, posted "Keep Off the Grass" signs, and made infractions of this rule punishable by fine.

Overlooking the Concert Ground on the Mall, the elegant Victorian-style Casino, designed by Calvert Vaux as an eatery for unescorted female visitors, had become a restaurant for both sexes. With the addition of a dance floor in the 1920s, it became a popular nightclub patronized by the Tammany Hall mayor, playboy, and songwriter James J. ("Gentleman Jimmy") Walker. Moses repudiated both the former administration (Walker had been thrown out of office in 1932 on charges of graft) and the current use of the building as an elite establishment. After tearing down the Casino in 1937, he converted the site into the Mary Harriman Rumsey Playground over the objections of civic groups who felt that, with twenty-two perimeter playgrounds, another in the middle of the park was unnecessary.

Moses's taste in public art soon became apparent. Instead of statues commemorating important figures in literary, cultural, and political history, he commissioned works of a whimsical nature, most of which were based on children's stories. In 1938 he used WPA funds to erect a granite statue of Mother Goose by Frederick George Richard Roth. With soaring cloak, she sits astride a flying goose at the entrance to the Rumsey Playground. The statue's bas-relief base depicts Little Jack Horner, Humpty Dumpty, and Little Bo Peep. Additionally, near the entrance to the Heckscher Playground, which Moses rebuilt in 1935, he placed a granite drinking fountain as a memorial to the child-welfare advocate Sophie Irene Loeb, which was sculpted with bas-reliefs of characters from *Alice in Wonderland*. In 1937 he had a playful pair of life-size bronzes, *Dancing Bear* and *Dancing Goat,* also by Roth, installed at the entrance to the zoo he had built to replace the park's old menagerie.

Tennis courts and a tennis house, built in 1930 according to the design of the park's chief engineer, Gustavo Steinacher, encroached on the South Meadow near the 96th Street Transverse Road. Before Moses this was the sole dedicated sports complex in the park. In 1934, during his first year in office, he turned the nearby North Meadow into ball fields and the adjacent stables into a recreation center, and he encircled the crest of the Great Hill with a wide path for roller-skating. Inside this asphalt ring, hard sand courts for roque, a version of croquet, were laid out, and wickets for regular croquet were set up on nearby lawns. During that same year, the sheepfold that housed the flock that grazed on Sheep Meadow was converted into the Tavern on the Green. Vaux's stable fronting the 86th Street Transverse Road became a police station, and the park was subsequently patrolled by officers charged with enforcing Moses's rules and regulations.

The Old Reservoir between the 79th and 86th Street Transverse Roads, which predated the park's creation, had been filled in during the 1920s when a new water tunnel made it obsolete. The American Society of Landscape Architects had prepared an axial plan in the Beaux-Arts style to turn the area into the Great Lawn, but it was not implemented until 1936, two years after Moses took office.

Its principal designer was Gilmore D. Clarke, Moses's chief land-scape architect for many years. Not long after its completion Moses decided that Clarke's grass oval should be converted into eight ball fields. In the north end of the park, Moses tore down the 1899 greenhouses near Fifth Avenue and 104th Street, which had for-merly been used for propagating park plant material, and directed Clarke to transform the six-acre site into the Conservatory Garden. As with the Great Lawn, Beaux-Arts symmetry prevailed. The gar-den has a central axial lawn bordered by allées of crabapples and is terminated by a fountain jet and a semicircle of hedges stepping up in tiers to a terrace crowned with a wisteria-covered wrought-iron pergola. A large circular garden on the north for seasonal display is balanced by a garden of geometrically arranged perennial beds on the south. In 1936, Bessie Potter Vonnoh's fountain sculpture of Mary and Dickon, the protagonists of Frances Hodgson Burnett's well-loved children's story *The Secret Garden*, was installed in the pool in the south garden. In 1947 the heirs of Samuel Untermyer donated the sculptor Walter Schott's 1910 fountain featuring jets of water splashing on bronze dancing maidens, which had formerly graced one of the lavish gardens at Greystone, Untermyer's 150-acre estate in Yonkers and now ornaments the pool in the north garden.

To make the park more actively family oriented, Moses staged events at the Naumburg Bandshell, which had been built in 1923 on the Concert Ground at the northern end of the Mall to replace the original cast-iron bandstand that had stood there. Here musical performances designed to attract a variety of ethnic groups were held, which included German, Gaelic, Polish, and Scottish song-fests. There were recitals conducted by the composer and cellist Victor Herbert, and the craze for big band music prompted the introduction of dance contests.

During the 1940s, as federal funds were directed toward the war effort, Moses was unable to lavish recreational facilities on the city as generously as when manpower was supplied by the federal pub-lic works programs of the Great Depression. But within the lim-its of the city budget, parks department engineers and the regular workforce were able to undertake a number of routine maintenance operations and perform small capital projects: the reseeding of lawns, the addition of asphalt paths and parking lots, and the repair of broken benches and lights. These improvements were intended to enhance security, increase safety, augment automobile access, and signal that management was on the job.

During this time, Moses filled in Ladies Pond, the most westerly arm of the Lake, and in 1941, when he had the 65th Street Cross Drive realigned for the convenience of automobile traffic, he buried Marble Arch, the pedestrian underpass leading to and from the Mall. He converted Cherry Hill Concourse, designed by Olmsted and Vaux as a carriage turnaround with an ornamental central fountain used for watering horses, into a parking lot. He marked the sites of the forts that had been built in the north end of the park by militiamen at the onset of the War of 1812 by installing flagpoles, pavement, benches, and commemorative plaques. Here, as elsewhere, nature lovers protested the destruction of the park's naturalistic character, but with no public accountability to restrict his authority, Moses was able to remove trees and pave over chosen areas with impunity.

To put it mildly, the architects, landscape architects, and engineers working in the parks department's Arsenal headquarters during the Moses years had a different aesthetic approach from that of the park's original nineteenth-century designers. They reengineered water bodies, rimming their edges with riprap and perimeter paths of asphalt, thereby destroying naturalistic shorelines fringed with emergent vegetation. The Harlem Meer, the placid lake near 110th Street, and the Pond in the southeast corner of the park near 59th Street received this treatment in the early 1940s.

Lewis Mumford, the most eminent architectural writer of the day, complained:

H. G. Wells once described Sidney Webb, the trenchant British bureaucrat, as the kind of person who would hack down growing trees and substitute sanitary green glass umbrellas. There is someone in the planning office of our Parks Department whose mind works the same way. Even in a romantic setting, he favors firm, manmade boundaries—iron fences, concrete curbs, heavy wooden barriers, devices that Olmsted and his architectural partner, Calvert Vaux, except in such formal layouts as the Mall, did their best to avoid. As for the borders of the lake, instead of planting them thickly with sedge and iris, the Parks Department designer has tried to combine beauty with ease of maintenance by planting them, too, with slabs of stone. The result is damnably neat, but that is about all, for the wide, asphalted paths and stone embankments completely counteract the natural loveliness of the landscape.[1]

Landscaping, if Moses's heavily engineered approach can be called that, was done in conjunction with the construction of the Wollman Rink on the northeastern arm of the Pond. To secure funding for this project, he found time to take walks in Central Park with Samuel J. Harris, a former New York Supreme Court justice and the lawyer for Kate Wollman, principal trustee of the William J. Wollman Foundation. With the help of his friend Harris, Moses persuaded Miss Wollman to give $600,000 toward the $800,000 cost of building the rink. Throughout the 1950s, Moses continued to combine private philanthropy with city appropriations to build other projects in Central Park: new structures for park concessions, public restrooms called comfort stations, more playgrounds, a new boathouse on the Lake, a rebuilt Carousel.

Moses adroitly steered prospective donors toward the kind of sculpture and architecture he liked and told artists and designers exactly what he wanted: playful statues and sound, functional, modern structures conservatively clothed and with touches of whimsy. Aymar Embury II, who had been recruited in 1934 along with Clarke to be a member of the parks department's newly formed design and construction department, was the principal author of this architectural idiom of disciplined playfulness. He and his team believed in using traditional materials of the highest quality, often brick and limestone in combination, or rough-hewn fieldstone with limestone trim. Attention to detail was important. A patterned surface com-

posed of alternating bands of brick and limestone masonry, a polygonal rather than rectilinear plan, and a peaked cupola to surmount
the central convergence of the right angles of a hip roof characterize
many small parks structures of the Moses period. These buildings
were built to be as sturdy and vandal-proof as the house of the wis-
est pig in "The Three Little Pigs."

In 1950 a fire destroyed the Carousel, a longtime favorite park
vendor-operated concession. Moses soon located a handsome forty-
year-old Coney Island carousel with horses carved of applewood by
the noted Brooklyn carousel makers Sol Stein and Harry Goldstein.
He had a new motor installed and, with a gift of $2,000, purchased
a Wurlitzer band organ. The park's director of mechanical maintenance oversaw the repainting of the carousel's fifty-seven prancing
steeds in what he called "real horsy colors." Moses obtained a gift
from the Michael Friedsam Foundation to erect the brick-and-lime-
stone-striped octagonal building that houses the carousel today.

The same year Moses turned to the financier, presidential
adviser, and statesman Bernard Baruch, whose favorite spot for discussing governmental affairs was a bench in Central Park, for funds
to build the Chess and Checkers House on the site previously occupied by the largest and most elaborate of the park's rustic summerhouses. In the meantime, the adjacent Dairy, one of Vaux's original
buildings, was converted into a storage depot for workers' tools and
supplies.

In 1954, when Jeanne Kerbs, who lived in an apartment house
overlooking the Conservatory Water near the corner of Fifth Avenue and 74th Street, wished to memorialize her parents, Moses
solicited her donation for the construction of a boathouse for model
yachts. Relatively small in scale, this typical Moses building has
brick walls with limestone quoins and a steeply pitched, gently
curving hip roof of copper crowned with a tall, thin, ornamental
cupola. Also in 1954, in order to replace the twenty-nine-year-old
wooden boathouse on the northeast arm of the Lake, Moses successfully sought funds from the investment banker Carl M. Loeb,
who donated $305,000, almost the entire amount needed to build
the boathouse that is named for him and his wife, Adeline. In 1957

he demolished another original park structure, the Mineral Springs Pavilion at the northwest corner of Sheep Meadow, replacing it with the present one built according to his standard brick-and-limestone design template.

In 1953, Moses accepted $75,000 raised by the Danish-American Women's Association for a bronze statue by Georg Lober to commemorate the 150th anniversary of Hans Christian Andersen's birth. His conservative taste for storybook sculpture was doubly apparent that year because of his vociferous opposition to a modern playground designed by the sculptor Isamu Noguchi for a site next to the new United Nations. Such was Moses's influence at this time that the plan was withdrawn, even though the Noguchi playground was not on city parkland. The Hans Christian Andersen sculpture, dedicated in 1956 and placed on the west side of the Conservatory Water opposite the Kerbs Model Yacht Boathouse, depicts the Ugly Duckling advancing toward the larger-than-life-size figure of the genial author, who is dressed in a frock coat and seated with an open book on his lap. The storyteller's knees and the invitingly spread pages of his book are now as shiny as a new penny where generations of climbing children have burnished their original bronze patina.

The northern end of the Conservatory Water received the last and best-loved piece of Moses-era sculpture, José de Creeft's *Alice in Wonderland,* given in 1959 by George T. Delacorte, the millionaire founder of the Dell Publishing Company, in memory of his wife, Margarita. The March Hare, Mad Hatter, and dormouse crowding around Alice, who is enthroned on a huge mushroom, resemble those in John Tenniel's illustrations for the original edition of Lewis Carroll's famous book. While they are clearly in character, the Mad Hatter possesses Delacorte's features, and Alice is thought to resemble de Creeft's daughter Donna. Although at least one art critic characterized Moses's taste in public art as puerile, the surface gleam of the mushroom and Alice's outstretched arms and fingers testify to the statue's perennial popularity.

In 1952 a memorial playground honoring William Church Osborn, a former president of the Metropolitan Museum of Art, was built at Fifth Avenue and 84th Street. Paul Manship designed its handsome bronze entrance gates depicting the Tortoise and the Hare, and the Wolf and the Lamb, along with other animals from Aesop's fables. The gates were removed when the playground was demolished in 1978 to make way for the Metropolitan Museum's addition to house the Temple of Dendur. They have recently been cleaned and repaired by the Central Park Conservancy and readied for installation at the entrance to the playground.

In 1957 the Irving and Estelle Levy Foundation provided funds for a small rectangular playground south of the Metropolitan Museum near the 79th Street Transverse Road. Like the Osborn Playground, it was furnished with standard play equipment—swings, slide, seesaws, sandbox—and entered through specially commissioned animal-ornamented bronze gates. A memorial to Irving Levy, they were designed by the sculptor A. Walter Beretta and architect John Wilson. When the playground was replaced in 1990 by the Pat Hoffman Friedman Playground situated closer to Fifth Avenue, the Levy gates were integrated into its design, along with Samuel Friedman's gift of Manship's 1960 *Group of Bears*.

Moses, who had served under several successive New York governors, encouraged Governor Herbert H. Lehman and his wife to donate the Lehman Children's Zoo located just north of the main Central Park Zoo in honor of the couple's fiftieth anniversary in 1961. Lehman had recently been elected governor when Moses built the original zoo in 1934 as an act of friendship toward his political patron, former governor Alfred E. Smith. Smith took great delight in walking from his apartment across Fifth Avenue to visit the iron-bar-caged exotic animals almost every day. By contrast, the enormously popular Lehman Children's Zoo was a juvenile stage set in which familiar farm animals were penned and petted. Manship's entrance gates depicting a youth dancing to the music of panpipes are of a much higher artistic quality than was the theme-park-like zoo, which was intelligently redesigned in 1996 when its operation was transferred to the Wildlife Conservation Society.

By the mid-1950s, Moses's arrogant sarcasm, political power, and press connections, which had previously withered opponents, intimidated mayors, and influenced reporters, were unable to mute the voices of those who could no longer tolerate his autocratic style. At the same time, his preference for landscape utility over scenery came under attack from the nascent environmental and historic preservation movements. While civic organizations, including the Parks Association of New York City, had raised objections to projects such as the Rumsey Playground with respectful diffidence in the 1930s, they now called Moses's continuing addition of recreational facilities to Central Park unwanted encroachments.

Things came to a dramatic head in 1955, when the newspapers announced that Moses wished to build an "Oldsters' Center" in the Ramble for persons over fifty-five. The project would transform the prevailing character of the twenty-two-acre woodland into a bland expanse of open lawns dotted with chess-and-checkers tables and areas for horseshoe pitching, croquet, and shuffleboard. The center was to be funded with a gift of $250,000 from the Albert and Mary Lasker Foundation and named in honor of Albert's sister, the social-welfare advocate Florina Lasker. Relandscaping the Ramble would be accomplished with $200,000 from the city budget. To do this Moses felt it necessary to fence the area. Serious bird-watchers would be allowed to enter in the early morning hours and "orderly adults" during the rest of the day. To prepare for the changes to come, paths were repaved and lined with London plane trees, standard parks department construction elements such as pipe railings and concrete retaining walls were installed, and a parking lot was built beside the East Drive.

But Moses underestimated the vehemence of the opposition to his plan. Located on the Atlantic flyway, the Ramble serves as a nesting ground for resident birds and refueling food source for migratory species. With dismissive contempt for the protesting bird-watchers, he was surprised when the Linnaean Society assembled enough strength and political backing to successfully oppose his plan to remove the area's existing vegetation. Perceiving a lack of support from the press and the strength of the political forces against him, Moses dropped the project, and the Lasker gift was withdrawn.

An even more contentious battle arose in 1956, with more lasting damage to Moses's reputation. Always at pains to increase the convenience of motorists in the park, he wished to supplement the existing parking at the Tavern on the Green with the addition of another eighty spaces. A group of mothers whose children played in the area got wind of his plans. On April 20 they angrily faced down the bulldozer operators beginning to clear the site of vegetation. Two days later they received the backing of the Citizens Union. Undeterred, Moses denied the mothers' request for a public hearing and, as a sop, offered their children the right to roller-skate on the parking lot before 5 p.m. On April 24 when the women arrived to protest, they found thirty workmen and twenty-five policemen with orders to restrain them from entering the area, which had been cordoned off with snow fencing overnight. The press, which for years had been in thrall to Moses's powerful public relations machinery, now saw the mothers up against the bulldozers as more than good copy: this was a story that showed that the parks hero they had lauded, the man who had been idolized by the public for so long, had feet of clay.

The next day, the *New York Times* revealed that "Commissioner Moses, though he did not personally supervise operations, commanded one bulldozer, one power shovel, two dump trucks, pneumatic drills, charges of dynamite, gasoline chain saws, pickaxes, shovels, axes, hatchets, and ropes." One mother was forcibly restrained by a policeman as a workman finished hacking down a tree, other women wept, and photographers took pictures of the scene.[2] While Moses brushed off the controversy as an inconsequential flap over a mere half-acre and a few trees, his publicity went from bad to worse. Better connected than the poor whose neighborhoods he displaced by slum-clearance projects elsewhere, the mothers had lawyer friends to help them obtain an injunction halting work pending a judicial hearing.

While Moses was on vacation, the opposition swelled. More reasons were found to oppose his heretofore unassailable authority over all parkland—authority he had helped write into the city charter. Recalling one of his reasons for tearing down the affordable

Casino in 1934, opponents argued that Tavern on the Green was a pricey restaurant that average park visitors could not afford to patronize. Moreover, parking spaces that benefited a private concessionaire were a questionable use of public parkland. A taxpayers' suit was filed. When Moses returned, he learned that the city's corporation counsel, Peter Campbell Brown, had worked out an arrangement with the mothers' attorney, Louis N. Field, to delay the case until the furor had subsided and Moses could announce that he was building a playground instead of a parking lot on the site. On July 18 the *Times* ran a story under the galling headline "Moses Yields to Mothers," quoting a compliment by the victorious Field: "Bob Moses has gone overboard and is going all out to do the right thing."

This was a public relations blow from which Moses's image as a great park builder never recovered. Two other humiliating defeats lay ahead. In 1954, Moses allowed Joseph Papp, the founder of the New York Shakespeare Festival, to hold performances in the park, but after agreeing to support the construction of a permanent summer theater, Moses subsequently backed away. Stuart Constable, the man he had appointed as the executive director of the parks department, started a smear campaign based on Papp's purported communism. Moses felt compelled to support Constable, and he now tried to block the project through a series of bureaucratic and budgetary maneuvers designed to make the theater, which he had originally been willing to fund with city money, unaffordable for Papp's shoestring organization.

But Papp, a child of the slums, was a skilled street fighter with a passionately democratic vision: free Shakespeare. He was able to garner extraordinarily favorable press and, like the playground mothers, he took Moses to court. The philanthropist George Delacorte decided to come to the rescue, and once more litigation was averted. On January 25, 1961, Newbold Morris, Moses's successor as parks commissioner, accepted the philanthropist's unsolicited gift of $150,000, the balance needed to supplement the $225,000 appropriation approved by the city's Board of Estimate. On June 18, 1962, the new 2,500-seat outdoor Delacorte Theater, situated beside the Belvedere Lake (today called Turtle Pond), opened with a benefit production of *The Merchant of Venice*. The funds collected would support the summer's free performances. Papp declared the event a people's victory, and Mayor Robert F. Wagner Jr. praised Papp's persistence.

In 1960, Moses made his last stand in Central Park in defense of a proposed gift from Huntington Hartford, the heir to the A&P supermarket fortune. Hartford wanted to build a café in the southeast corner of the park, and Moses agreed to accept a design by the architect Edward Durrell Stone, described as "a flat-topped double-decker of concrete, with sliding glass doors that can be opened on the park side and along the 59th Street sidewalk." Intended to serve five hundred diners on each of its two levels, it would have a footprint of 240 by 40 feet.[3]

Four civic organizations protested, but Moses reminded them that the city charter gave the parks commissioner the authority to accept gifts without the approval of any other city official. Nevertheless, Walter Hoving, the chairman of Tiffany & Co., and a group of fellow merchants filed a lawsuit protesting the park incursion. Giving voice to the growing notion of Moses as an autocrat, Hoving declared: "Some officials in office a long time seem to get a sovereignty complex. Not only do they feel they know better than the rest of us taxpayers, but they ride roughshod sometimes, notably Robert Moses, whose fine work for many years I have applauded, but whose habitual arrogance, particularly in this situation, I decry."[4] By this time Moses was on the verge of retiring as parks commissioner in order to serve as coordinator of the 1964 World's Fair in Flushing Meadows Park. Newbold Morris and his successors were therefore left to deal with the café fight and the building of the park's last large-scale Moses-era recreation facility, the Lasker Rink and Pool.

With regard to Huntington Hartford's café, the state's Court of Appeals, which had long upheld the authority over all parks-related matters given to the parks commissioner by the City Charter, did not do so now. On April 27, 1962, it handed down an affirmative verdict for the prosecution that marked the beginning of citizen

protection of Central Park as a scenic landscape. Hartford, however, did not give up his dream of bringing a Parisian-style sidewalk
café to New York. He directed Stone to modify the design in the
hope that the project might still go forward, but the election of John
V. Lindsay as mayor in 1965 sealed its doom. A month after Lindsay
took office, his young parks commissioner, Thomas Pearsall Field
Hoving, son of Walter Hoving, declared, "We just have to be res-
olute about some things. One, two, three—bang!" Hartford complained, "Moses suggested the location and he is a very great man.
He knew the park a hell of a lot better than anyone else."[5] Hoving
tried to persuade Hartford to redirect his $800,000 gift to his own
pet project, the building of twenty vest-pocket parks in low-income
neighborhoods, but Hartford declined, and on March 4, 1966,
Hoving asked the city comptroller to return Hartford's money.

At the opposite end of the park, however, the $2.6 million com-
bined rink and pool proposed as a memorial to Albert and Florina
Lasker's sister Loula, for which the Albert and Mary Lasker Foundation had provided $600,000, went forward at the mouth of the
Loch, the stream that empties into the Harlem Meer after flowing
through the scenic ravine traversing the northern end of the park.
Although it would prove as popular in the summer as the other big,
well-managed swimming pools Moses had lavished on the city and
in the winter give skaters a less crowded alternative to the Wollman
Rink, this intrusion presented a dire contrast to the area's sylvan
scenery. This time, however, the protests of park preservationists
were ineffectual. When the rink was dedicated on December 21,
1966, Mayor Lindsay and Thomas Hoving, the self-declared enemy
of Robert Moses's park encroachments, took a whirl on the ice.

Thirty-three New Ways You Can Help Central Park's Renaissance

(1983)

Seven years ago, with New York City's finances at a precarious point, there was no more potent symbol of the city's near collapse than Central Park. The trees were dying for lack of care, and acres of lawn had been pounded into hardpan. The fountains had gone dry, the buildings were rotting, and the staff was demoralized.

It was clear that City Hall didn't—or *couldn't*—care for the park, except superficially, and it would be two years before Edward Koch would become mayor and appoint as parks commissioner a politically inspired and managerially adept lawyer and city planner, Gordon Davis. Temporary federal funds enabled the parks department to hire back some of the employees it had been forced to fire. But the "make do" approach adopted by a series of short-term commissioners offered little hope for the future.

At the time, some friends and I formed a nonprofit corporation—the Central Park Task Force—to encourage private donations for a host of park-improvement projects the city was unable to address. To publicize this initiative, I wrote an article titled "32 Ways Your Time or Money Can Rescue Central Park" for the June 14, 1976, issue of *New York*. Among the listings: "Refurbish the Dairy ($350,000)"; "Fund a summer intern ($700)"; Restore a shrub bed ($100)." The response was overwhelming. Letters and checks

From *New York*, June 6, 1983.

poured in. Within two weeks we had received $25,000 and—equally gratifying—scores of wonderful reminiscences about the park from devoted users.

For the next two years, the Central Park Task Force that I headed continued to raise money for the park. During the same period, another organization, the Central Park Community Fund, was carrying on similar efforts. Then, in 1978, after the election of Edward I. Koch as mayor, Gordon Davis became parks commissioner, and in order to help reform the park's management and oversee capital projects for the restoration of its decrepit architectural features and nearly destroyed landscapes, he created the position of Central Park administrator. "You know," he told me when he asked me to accept the job, "you'll have to raise your own money to hire staff and to do many of the things you want to do."

Davis, who recently stepped down from office and was succeeded by Henry Stern, was effective in winning for the parks department additional city resources, but he was no magician. The Central Park Task Force and the Central Park Community Fund continued to work with the new administrator's office, but it was clear that to be truly effective the two groups should merge. And so, in the fall of 1980, the Central Park Conservancy was founded. William S. Beinecke, the recently retired head of Sperry & Hutchinson, accepted Mayor Koch's invitation to form its board of directors. These included members of the two existing private park-support groups, as well as community leaders whose diversity reflected Central Park's democratic character.

From its inception, the Conservancy boldly presented itself as a candidate for serious philanthropy, one among several great New York City institutions, including Lincoln Center, the New York Zoological Society, the two botanical gardens, and numerous museums. We sought to inspire the people who lived around the park to think about what their glorious views were worth to them, and at the same time we knocked on the doors of corporate headquarters, pointing out to CEOs the value of the park to their employees.

Exxon came forward with funds for a program called "Double Your Green"—a dollar-for-dollar match of contributions by neighboring community groups for the replanting of deteriorated nearby park landscapes. Chase Manhattan Bank and the W. Alton Jones Foundation underwrote a $100,000 program to equip and train a corps of mounted urban park rangers. Bankers Trust Company gave $65,000 for a graffiti-removal program. And over $330,000 was collected from roughly nine thousand other groups and individuals.

With this kind of support supplementing city capital funds, Belvedere Castle has been restored and is now being operated by the Conservancy as a place for children's entertainment and education; the Bethesda and USS *Maine* Monument fountains are working again, as are the ones in the Conservatory Garden; Bethesda Terrace is being rebuilt; and next winter skaters will again enjoy gliding over smooth ice on Wollman Memorial Rink. In fact, almost all of the thirty-two projects listed in the 1976 *New York* article have been completed.

Promising as all of this is, it is only a beginning. While some of the most obvious deterioration is being reversed, the overall fabric of the park has yet to receive sufficient attention. Few people realize that Central Park is *entirely* man-made. Regrading, soil enrichment, and the planting of new grass and groundcovers are absolutely essential to stop erosion and ensure a green ecosystem. An extensive drainage infrastructure already exists to prevent low-lying areas from becoming boggy once again, but it needs thorough—and expensive—repairs.

The park's original designers, Frederick Law Olmsted and Calvert Vaux, conceived a brilliant and ingenious circulation system of carriage drives, bridle trails, pedestrian paths, and sunken east–west crosstown transverse roads, but inappropriate alterations over the years plus increased traffic have made certain revisions necessary. The park's trees, many of which are of arboretum quality and variety, need continuous care, and new trees must be planted. A Conservancy-funded team of planners is currently studying and analyzing the work that will need to be done in Central Park over the next ten years. This effort will result in a management and restoration plan that will guide future capital projects and management budgets.

Even as the experts try to integrate the elements of the plan with the imperatives of history, aesthetics, and social demand, there are immediate projects to be implemented. Indeed, Central Park needs help now as much as it did seven years ago. The city is in a continuing struggle for fiscal stability, and little help can be expected from Albany or Washington. It is up to New Yorkers to save Central Park. Here are thirty-three *more* ways you can do it.

1. Replant a Shoreline
To prevent future erosion, special attention must be paid to stream embankments and shorelines.
- Plant 500 linear feet of water's edge with aquatic
  vegetation and wetland shrubs $2,000

2. Repair a Boat Landing
The three rustic boat landings beside the Lake, near 72nd Street, need periodic repairs.
- Pay for the lumber and hardware $1,500

3. Rebuild a Rustic Shelter
Summerhouses, gazebos, and arbors artfully constructed of interlocking tree logs once dotted the park landscape, providing comfortable places to read or enjoy the view. The Conservancy's restoration crew has repaired the only surviving rustic shelter in the Ramble (there used to be fifteen in this section of the park alone) with funds provided by Arthur Ross (a philanthropist who is also a Conservancy trustee). With a grant from an anonymous donor, they have also built, on the flat surface of the top of the bedrock outcrop overlooking the Dene—a small grassy valley at 67th Street near Fifth Avenue—a historically faithful replica of the rustic shelter torn down by Moses. It is time now to reconstruct the Cop Cot, a rustic gazebo atop another bedrock knoll near the Sixth Avenue entrance, and repair the Wisteria Pergola next to the Mall.
- Pay for the rebuilding of the Cop Cot $75,000
- Pay for the lumber, pavers, and ironwork necessary
  to restore the Wisteria Pergola $80,000

4. Restore a Stone Stairway

Carefully inserted into the park's hilly terrain are nearly a hundred sets of stone stairways. Most were installed when the park was built in the nineteenth century; since that time the heaving action of frost, the slow, relentless pressure of soil against stone, and the penetration of tree roots into the subsoil have undermined them. The set of stairs at 102nd Street and Fifth Avenue is in particularly deplorable condition, as is the nearby perimeter wall built of the park's native rock, Manhattan schist. The restoration crew can rebuild several sets of interior stairs and repair the exterior wall if funds for masonry and mortar are provided.

- Buy supplies and equipment to rebuild the steps and repair the park wall at 102nd Street $80,000
- Realign and repoint a set of stone stairs $2,000

5. Hire a Preservation-Crew Apprentice

Trained masons and skilled carpenters are required if the park's restored stone, brick, and wooden features are to be well-maintained and not to fall into disrepair once more. The Conservancy wants to provide young people with career opportunities that will also be of benefit to the park. We need your help in order to offer training, supervision, and salaries for these new members of our workforce.

- Hire a preservation-crew apprentice for one year $19,500

6. Replant a Park Entrance

Because they sustain a heavy amount of human and canine traffic, the park entrances need periodic replanting with hardy shrubs. Help raise money from your neighbors or block association and Exxon's "Double Your Green" program will match it.

- Replant a typical park entrance $6,000

7. Computerize Park Tree Care

A Central Park tree inventory, conducted between May 15 and October 1, 1982, has classified and assessed the condition of every tree in the park over six inches in diameter—25,000 trees in all. The survey is the first of its kind and will be used as a working model for inventories in other cities throughout the country. With this data now loaded onto a mainframe, our tree inventory is both a historic document and a management tool. Based on information gathered on the size, type, condition, and location of each tree, we may now track the health of both newly planted trees and venerable old ones. Such a system can greatly increase the productivity of the Conservancy's specialized tree-care crew.

- Fund a computer terminal $3,500
- Fund two summer jobs for graduate students in
  forestry to update the tree inventory $5,000

8. Plant a Wildflower Meadow
Two years ago, when we began the search for ways to reduce park maintenance expenses without sacrificing landscape beauty, we started to experiment with mixtures of wildflowers and native grasses on slopes and in glades where foot traffic is light. The now-blooming Queen Anne's lace, sunflowers, daisies, goldenrod, and black-eyed Susans in these meadows offer the same experience as an open field or country roadside in the middle of Manhattan. We want to bring more of this wild horticulture to the park.

- Plant one acre with wildflower seed $750

9. Help Develop Tough Turf
During the past year we have been learning a great deal from golf course managers and athletic-field specialists about the proper soil composition and grass-seed mixtures necessary to maintain strong turf on ball fields and other grassy areas used for sports. We have already secured sufficient funds to re-sod the East Meadow at 97th Street and the East Green at 71st Street, but many remaining bare, soil-compacted portions of the park landscape need the same kind of renovation.

- Buy one acre of turf and provide for the management
  necessary to get it established $8,000

10. Hire a Horticulturist
Reviving and maintaining the park's flora require the skills of

trained horticulturists. Although some landscaping projects are being accomplished by outside contractors, we have begun to increasingly rely on our own landscape-restoration crew, which is now jointly funded by the parks department and the Conservancy. As more sections of the park are improved, we need to expand the size of the Conservancy's landscaping reconstruction and horticultural maintenance teams. A five-person watering crew is necessary during the spring and fall planting seasons, and the personnel that make up the turf and tree-care crews must be supplemented if we are to realize our 1983 goal of restoring thirty-five acres of lawn with grass and five entrances and their surrounding landscapes with new flowering trees and ornamental shrubs.

- Hire a recent graduate of the SUNY School of
  Horticulture for a year $17,000

11. Save the Elms

During the past fifty years, the American elm has come to be regarded as not just a tree but a national arboreal treasure. The 1920s saw an outbreak of Dutch elm disease, which destroyed almost all of the American elms that once graced college campuses and New England village greens. Many of those in Central Park fortunately survived the epidemic, and the park now boasts the largest stand of elms in the entire Northeast—nearly 2,000. These include 507 planted as street trees along the Fifth Avenue perimeter of the park and the 258 that form the four allées bordering the Mall. The success of the function of the latter as the park's single formal design element was forecast by the nineteenth-century diarist George Templeton Strong, an observant note-taker on the park's construction, who saw the Mall soon after it had been planted. Describing it as a "broad avenue, exceptionally straight, . . . with a quadruple row of elms," he predicted that it "will look Versailles-y by A.D. 1950."[1]

The American elms on the Mall with their overarching branches today form a vaulted, cathedral-like ceiling. yet without a program of Dutch-elm-disease control to keep the survivors free of bark infection by the species of beetle that serves as a vector, the

Mall could be nearly a clear, flat space within five to seven years. Therefore, annually before the elms bud, they must be sprayed with nontoxic dormant oil, which suffocates the eggs of the bark beetle. Then, for the three months between June 1 and September 1 the Conservancy's tree crew must monitor the elms, checking daily for evidence of disease. Dead and beetle-infected wood must be pruned. Where possible, the elms must be injected with fungicide, but some seriously distressed trees must be felled. With such a program of arboreal sanitation, Dutch elm disease can be checked, and the mortality rate of the 10 to 20 percent of elms that have lacked sufficient care can be reduced to 1 or 2 percent.

- Inject an elm with fungicide $50
- Prune a diseased tree $150
- Provide funds for an all-day consultation with a tree
  pathologist $200

12. Preserve the Heritage Trees

Many of the trees planted in Central Park by Olmsted and Vaux were not suited to the environment and have long since vanished. Others have flourished, including several exotic varieties, such as the Turkey oak and Chinese elm, and trees otherwise unknown in urban areas, such as the American beech. There are over two hundred trees scattered throughout Central Park that are classified as historic because of their age, size, unusual configuration, landscape placement, or rarity in this country. Many of these trees are almost one hundred years old and are now performing fully their roles as envisioned in the park's nineteenth-century Greensward plan. All of these trees are irreplaceable. If the historic trees are not maintained on a regular basis, they will deteriorate and eventually disappear.

- Prune, fertilize, cable, and brace (where necessary)
  five heritage trees $1,500

13. Prune Playground Trees for Safety

Dead overhanging tree limbs are a hazard no matter where they are found in the park, but they are particularly dangerous in playgrounds. Playgrounds should be inspected and dangerous limbs removed on a regular basis.

- Prune trees in a typical playground $1,500

14. Fertilize for Health and Beauty

If Central Park's many varieties of trees are to flourish and withstand the particularly punishing stress of urban park conditions, they need extra help. They benefit greatly from periodic fertilization.

- Fertilize 200 newly planted trees $2,000
- Prune and fertilize a venerable specimen tree $150

15. Re-Green the Great Lawn

Originally the site of one of the Croton Aqueduct's receiving reservoirs, the Great Lawn today is a series of baseball diamonds rimmed on the southeast and west by Manhattan's romantic skyline of towers and spires, while to the north there is nothing but that most precious of all New York City commodities—a huge open sky. Here, in the long afternoons of late spring, summer, and early fall, and all day Saturday and Sunday, regular and impromptu ball teams gather to play. Because of its size (fourteen acres) the Great Lawn can also accommodate such large-scale events as the regularly scheduled performances by the New York Philharmonic and the Metropolitan Opera; occasional once-in-a-lifetime pop musical celebrations as exemplified by the Barbra Streisand comeback concert and the Simon and Garfunkel reunion; and officially permitted free-speech political protests like last year's antinuclear rally.

With the help of city funds, the popular Heckscher ball fields at the park's southern end have recently been covered with a blanket of new sod and are now receiving proper maintenance by the Conservancy's turf management team. Unfortunately, the same is not yet the case with the Great Lawn, which still needs to be turned from an eroded dusty plain back into a unified grassy expanse containing nine baseball diamonds. The Astor Foundation has provided funds for engineering and landscape plans. These have shown us what needs to be done and how to do it. But there are as yet no funds available for the actual work of regrading, installation of proper drainage and irrigation infrastructure, soil aeration and enrichment, and laying new sod.

- Fund the re-greening of the Great Lawn $1.5 million

16. Plant Tomorrow's Trees

To compensate for inevitable losses, the park needs between sixty and seventy new trees of four-to-six-inch caliper each year. Our recent survey shows that we have a small aging population of river birches, beeches, tupelos, ironwoods, and hickories; we would like to replant more trees of the same species to ensure their continuing presence and park visitors' enjoyment of arboreal variety in the park in the future.

- Plant a four-to-six-inch-caliper tree $600
- Replant five trees of a disappearing species $3,000

17. Help the Conservatory Garden

The invisible line that transects Manhattan at 96th Street is a psychological barrier that prevents many people from experiencing one of the park's greatest treasures: the Conservatory Garden at 104th Street and Fifth Avenue. The entrance to the Garden is through the wrought-iron Vanderbilt Gates at Fifth Avenue and 104th Street, and from here the eye is directed into the park by an axially aligned rectangular greensward bordered by yew hedges and twin crabapple allées. At its western edge a circular fountain spouts a tall jet of water, beyond which rises a tier of terraced hedges topped by a wisteria-shaded pergola. Allées of crabapples border this central section, next to which on the north and on the south are separate gardens with bronze sculptural fountains and flower beds.

In 1979, under the auspices of the Central Park Task Force, the replanting of the Conservatory Garden was undertaken by the New York Committee of the Garden Club of America, whose members organized a series of planting days and helped raise funds to repair the broken fountains. After its founding the following year, the Central Park Conservancy assumed responsibility for overseeing the garden's restoration, and Lynden Miller, an abstract artist–cum-gardener, produced a master plan for the restoration of its planting beds and repair of its broken bluestone path pavers. Under Miller's supervision, Conservancy interns began to weed and tend it, and in 1982 the Friends of the Conservatory Garden was formed as a volunteer horticultural workforce to tend the newly planted garden beds. At the same time, the Conservancy sought to interest bordering institutions, including Mount Sinai Medical Center, the Museum of the City of New York, and the Museo del Barrio, to bring yet more volunteers and community life into this aesthetically uplifting and spiritually therapeutic section of Central Park.

- Fund garden perennials for one large flower bed $750
- Repair the stairways leading to the wisteria pergola $7,500

18. Restore the Marionette Theatre

The Swedish Cottage is a relic of the 1876 Centennial Exhibition, the World's Fair in Philadelphia celebrating America's hundredth anniversary as a nation. Following its removal from the fairgrounds after the closing of the exposition, it was transported to Central Park where it has since continued to serve as a marionette theater, attracting families and groups of schoolchildren from all over the city. Its charming storybook architecture is appealing at first glance, but a closer look shows that, like many other park structures now undergoing repair, it is shabby and deteriorated. Worse, at present it does not comply with the city's fire code, nor does it provide adequate access for handicapped children.

- Underwrite the Swedish Cottage restoration $350,000

19. Rebuild or Repair a Playground

Central Park has nineteen playgrounds, varying in style from WPA Standard to Adventurous Modern. Because they are the most intensively used places in the park, they must be repaired frequently. Moreover, the ones at East 76th Street, East 108th Street, and West 81st Street are in need of complete renovation.

- Rebuild a playground $500,000
- Contribute to the Playground Repair Fund   any amount

20. Rebuild the Soil

When the construction of Central Park began in 1858, hundreds of thousands of cubic yards of topsoil were brought in by horse-drawn carts from New Jersey and Long Island. In the early years of the park's reconstruction fertilizer was added regularly and manure from nearby stables was composted and used to enrich its organic composition.

Now, after a hundred years of neglect, the park's soil is again receiving attention. The first soil study of an urban park in the United States was begun in Central Park in the spring of 1981 and completed in August 1982. As a result of data collected in this survey, soil erosion levels can be monitored and accurate decisions made about soil care. At present, the horticultural staff has no laboratory from which the Conservancy's soil monitoring and treatment programs can be run, and thus they suffer from delays in testing samples and reporting results by being forced to seek these services from agricultural laboratories outside New York City. A properly equipped soil laboratory in Central Park will make this basic component of our horticultural operations more efficient.

Composting, a practice that was once routine but was abandoned after the turn of the century, was reinstituted by the Conservancy four years ago on an experimental basis at the Mount, originally the site of the Academy of Mount Saint Vincent.[2] The now archaeological site, on land formerly owned by the Sisters of Charity of Saint Vincent de Paul until its acquisition by New York City in 1857 for the creation of Central Park, forms a steep hill behind the Conservatory Garden at the top of which there are now several large piles of decomposing leaves that grow smaller with each rainfall. Every area of the park in which new planting is being undertaken requires composted leaf mold from this source in order to enrich depleted soil, promote root growth, and supply nitrogen to the heritage and specimen trees throughout the park. In order to further develop the composting operation at the Mount, we need to install vehicular paths and buy additional equipment.

- Fund a soil-testing laboratory $7,500
- Fund interim off-site soil-testing operations for one year $5,000

- Underwrite lab construction $10,000
- Purchase necessary mechanical equipment to mix
  organic debris with loam and other nutrient ingredients
  to form compost piles $20,000
- Provide funds for the production of 1,000 cubic yards
  of compost $6,500

21. Keep the Fountains Flowing

The park's fine ornamental fountains at the USS *Maine* Monument, Bethesda Terrace, Cherry Hill, and the Conservatory Garden have all been repaired, and only the Pulitzer Fountain in front of the Plaza Hotel remains broken and dry. Its repair and nighttime lighting will dramatically enhance the appearance of the park's principal entrance.

To keep all the ornamental fountains as well as the public toilets, lawn-sprinkler systems, and drinking fountains in good repair, Central Park needs one additional full-time plumber.

- Restore and light up the Pulitzer Fountain $350,000
- Hire a plumber for one year $25,000
- Buy plumbing equipment and supplies $5,000

22. Put New Life into the Old Castle

Romantic folly-cum-weather station on Vista Rock above the 79th Street Transverse Road, the park's charming Victorian-style turreted three-story castle-like structure, originally christened the Belvedere because of its beautiful views of the park and the distant environs of the city and beyond, had deteriorated to such a state through neglect and vandalism that it was in danger of collapse. This is no longer true. Grants from the Astor Foundation and the Coles Foundation plus a $1.4 million capital budget allocation from the city of New York have returned the Belvedere, which is built of the park's Manhattan schist bedrock, to its original appearance. Exterior lighting has been provided by the Mertz Gilmore Foundation and interior furnishings by the Charles Hayden Foundation, Time Inc., and the Sperry Corporation. Under an agreement with the parks department, the Conservancy operates the Belvedere as an educational center. Here visitors can learn about the park's glacially scoured metamorphic rocks; the work performed by the meteorologists assigned to the US weather station for New York City who compile the daily reports from data collected by climatic measuring instruments located in a small fenced compound just south of the castle; and how to identify some of the 269 species of migratory and resident birds that visit or live in the park. Salaries for the Belvedere manager, an environmental educator, and a designated Belvedere ranger to act as a park guide are important ongoing funding requirements. Funds are also needed to improve the nighttime security system.

- Fund staff salaries for one year:
  - Belvedere manager $21,600
  - Environmental-education specialist $15,000
  - Belvedere ranger $15,000
- Fund a storyteller, mime, or puppeteer to provide a weekend performance at the Belvedere $150
- Fund an environmental-education workshop $500
- Fund a medieval concert by strolling troubadours $250
- Fund a geologist, ornithologist, or historian to lead a free public tour $150

23. Erase Graffiti

In 1982 grants from Bankers Trust Company and the Lillia Babbitt Hyde Foundation provided funds for the Conservancy's purchase of the chemicals and equipment that allowed it to integrate a three-person graffiti-removal team into its regular maintenance workforce. A remarkable 15,000 square feet of graffiti were expunged from walls, playgrounds, benches, fountains, monuments, and other areas of the park within a six-month period. Some graffitists' cartoon art and signature tags reappeared, but these, too, were promptly deleted.

Perhaps nothing signals to the public a safe and well-kept park more than an absence of graffiti, and we need more funds to make our initial success a permanent reality.

- Pay for the elimination of ten square feet of graffiti $70
- Hire a graffiti-removal intern for one year $17,500

24. Repair a Row of Benches

Each park bench has eight slats, and each slat costs $3.85. Hundreds of slats need to be replaced, repaired, and repainted every year by Conservancy and parks department maintenance crews and volunteers.

- Repair an entire park bench $30.80

25. Toss in a Trash Barrel

We need a fresh supply of two hundred trash barrels every year to replace losses due to damage and theft.

- Purchase one barrel $32.50

26. Help Keep the Five Conservancy Rangers Mounted

For nearly two years, five mounted rangers have been patrolling Central Park on horses purchased by the Conservancy. An investment in the continuing care of these horses and the training and equipment of their riders is repaid many times over by the friendly presence and increased safety they provide.

- Shoe one mounted-ranger horse for one year $460
- Adapt six police radios for ranger use $570
- Provide veterinary care for one horse for one year $350
- Replace five saddle blankets $225
- Buy one saddlebag for a portable first-aid kit $50
- Buy one new bridle $90
- Buy one new saddle $550
- Purchase one horse $2,000

27. Construct a Radio Command Center for Park Rangers and Night-Security Personnel

The remodeling of a currently unused portion of the recreation building at 97th Street to serve as home base and radio command post for our mounted rangers and night-security personnel will increase park safety. Their sequential work shifts over a twenty-four-hour period allows for sufficient space to enable another portion of the building to be converted into a small stable. One of the ensuing results of this remodeling will be substantial savings for the Conservancy, which currently must rent horse stalls outside the park. Citibank has given $52,000 toward the design of an entirely on-site mounted ranger facility, and other corporations and foundations have donated $57,000 to date for the creation of this equestrian-patrol necessity. Still more funding is needed to make the building an effective well-equipped command center for the mounted rangers' day-to-day operations.

- Provide the additional funds needed for the complete
  of the building at 97th Street as a park-security
  headquarters $280,000

28. Buy a Backstop or a Baseball Diamond
Wear and tear on the park by athletic activities necessitates constant renewal of required facilities. Ball fields in particular demand ongoing annual maintenance.

- Repair a backstop $300
- Furnish 50 yards of clay for one diamond $895

29. Make Us More Mechanically Efficient
Even with reduced park personnel, we can do the job if we have the needed equipment.

- Buy a clamdigger to clean out catch basins $35,000
- Buy a backhoe $35,000
- Purchase a snowblower $4,000
- Purchase a leaf vacuum $20,000
- Fund a forklift $18,000

30. Engage a Mechanic
Keeping the dump trucks, packer-loaders, leaf vacuums, garbage collectors, water trucks, rototillers, vans, tractors, and trucks in good working order—to say nothing of sharpening the blades of five lawn mowers—is a full-time job. At present, Central Park maintenance equipment and vehicles must be sent to the parks department's Five Borough Maintenance Shop on Randall's Island for repair. There they sit, alongside broken equipment and malfunctioning motor vehicles from other parts of the city, often for several

weeks or months at a time until the park department's mechanics are able to get around to repairing them. For this reason a Conservancy-sponsored mechanic assigned to work in Central Park is badly needed to keep our equipment rolling.

- Provide a mechanic's salary plus benefits for one year $26,000

31. Help Build the Future by Buying the Past

The rebuilding of Central Park demands historical research and the assembly of archival material that helps us envision the original park and gain knowledge of how it became what it is today. Photographic copies must be made of deteriorating maps and drawings to preserve them for future consultation by historians and landscape designers. In addition, the Conservancy's archivist is collecting dated photos, vintage magazine and newspaper stories, anecdotal letters, and diary entries relating to historic events and the physical changes that have occurred in the park.

- Fund one photograph of a historic document $50
- A visit to our office to share a dated photo, postcard, or
  family archive containing Central Park memorabilia $0.00

32. Lend a Hand by Counting Heads

In early June we will be conducting what we have named the Great Central Park Count. This will allow us to determine our daily and seasonal demographics, map the destinations of our multiple constituencies, and plot the most heavily used origin-and-destination routes.

- Contact the Conservancy to volunteer your participation for
  one day in the counting of visitors entering the park.
- Supply T-shirts, maps, pencils, clipboards, hand
  counters, trained personnel, and computer time $5,000

33. Help the Park without Spending a Dime

The renaissance of Central Park requires a regeneration of respect among its millions of users. Over the next decade, approximately $100 million will be spent to make the park as clean and safe and beautiful as it once was—a worthy centerpiece of the great city around it. You can help not only in big ways but also in small. Show you care. Stay on the park paths. Using paved pathways instead of lawns and other planted areas helps curtail erosion by allowing vegetation to thrive. Clean up after your dog. Leash your dog and maintain a respect for newly planted areas. Deposit trash in trash cans instead of dropping your candy wrapper, empty soft-drink bottle, or piece of used Kleenex on the ground. This form of considerate visitor behavior permits park workers to spend more time on activities related to rebuilding the landscape and improving the overall management of Central Park.

Jane and Me

(2016)

Let's say that I have been a Jane Jacobite since 1961, the year that *The Death and Life of Great American Cities* was published. It is certain that, if you asked me to name the five most influential books in my life, this would be on the list. For those of you gathered in this beautifully restored synagogue tonight, I will explain this by telling you some of my life story. Like most of my Wellesley contemporaries, immediately upon graduation I married my college boyfriend, thereupon becoming Mrs. Edward Barlow in 1957. Four years later, after Ed's stint in the Navy as a reserve officer, he applied for admission to Yale Law School. It was at this time that I avidly read Jane's iconoclastic book.[1] I knew then that I wanted to steer my life's course in the direction of her brand of urban improvement, and as a result, in 1962, once our daughter Lisa was enrolled in kindergarten in New Haven, I decided the time had come for me to enroll as a student in the Yale School of City Planning.

The date is important. Let's consider the term "*master* planning," a concept I dislike, which along with transportation engineering dominated the curriculum of city planning graduate programs like that at Yale. The school's proximity to a spur of the New England

Speech delivered on June 15, 2016, as part of the Jane Jacobs Centennial Lecture Series, organized by Roberta Gratz and the Center for the Living City, held at the Eldridge Street Synagogue in Manhattan's Lower East Side. A video recording is available at centerforthelivingcity.org.

Expressway carrying highway traffic into the center of New Haven south of College Green and the Yale campus offered in plain sight a perfect illustration of the reason for Jane's animus for the routing of thruways through downtowns and the razing of old neighborhoods with a healthy mix of local stores and friendly neighbors. So this was what master planners called urban renewal! Jane's particular nemesis was, of course, the biggest master planner of them all, Robert Moses.

In New Haven I could see the heavy footprint of another master planner, Edward Logue, who was responsible for the makeover of a significant part of that city. I learned that modernism (or modern, as it was still called) didn't apply only to architecture. It was also the predominant theory of urban planning at the time. Much as I admired the recently built Seagram Building standing in solitary splendor on its raised platform on Park Avenue, Le Corbusier's *Ville radieuse* was another matter. This architectural theorist's drawings of superblocks, detached from the richly textured urban fabric surrounding them, were, as Jane forcefully maintained, depictions of social demise in terms of city life. By contrast, her vision of a vibrant neighborhood was one comprised of low-scale older buildings with mixed uses. To experience this paradigm firsthand I had only to visit the pizza-heaven of Wooster Square a few blocks away.

At Yale I had a wonderful teacher of the history of cities, Christopher Tunnard, and I loved his cultural and architectural survey course. But you can imagine how popular I was with my other professors when I tried to incorporate into our studio assignments some of the ideals I had gained from *Death and Life of Great American Cities*. Strict zoning codes and the separation of city neighborhoods according to land-use plans were the accepted order of the day. I can remember the color-coded maps showing industrial zones in purple, commercial centers (CBDs, or central business districts) in red, and residential areas in yellow. There were some areas in green on these maps, but they seemed to be low-priority residual spaces rather than anything resembling in-town parks like the squares that had been created when Philadelphia and Savannah were laid out or the armatures for further growth as in the case of New York City,

Buffalo, and Boston, nineteenth-century cities where landscape architecture and city planning were indistinguishable, thanks to the visionary designs of Frederick Law Olmsted.

In Professor Tunnard's course I learned about the British garden city movement led by Ebenezer Howard and Raymond Unwin, a form of low-density urbanism in which people lived in close proximity both to one another and to nature, and how the garden city planning philosophy was adopted in this country in the early years of the twentieth century. Because Ed's parents lived in Forest Hills Gardens, the Queens semi-suburban community designed by Frederick Law Olmsted Jr., I had on our visits to them a firsthand experience of its curvilinear circulation system, ample lawns, and community center and parks for social and recreational neighborhood assembly.

Sunnyside Gardens, another planned community in the borough of Queens, was also within easy subway-riding distance. This example of green urbanism had grown out of the early-1920s vision of Lewis Mumford, the renowned literary critic, progressivist social philosopher, and cultural historian, whose chief books and essays focused on architecture, technological development, and urban design. It was due in large part to Mumford's advocacy of the principles of the English garden city movement that Sunnyside was designed by the architects Clarence Stein and Frederick Ackerman, the planner Henry Wright, and the landscape architect Marjorie Sewell Cautley. Each residence had a small front garden facing the street and a terrace overlooking a garden in the rear.

·

I have to say that, much as I admire Jane's brand of urbanism, I lean toward the philosophical view of Robert Kanigel, the author of a generally admiring biography of Jane, who believes that Mumford had a point in his scathing, overly contemptuous, and on the whole unfair review of *Death and Life* in which he maintains, "Her simple formula does not suggest that her eyes have ever been hurt by ugliness, sordor, confusion, or her ears offended by the roar of trucks smashing through a once quiet residential neighborhood, or her nose assaulted by the chronic odors of ill-ventilated, unsunned housing." Kanigel points out that Jane loathed Sunnyside because she thought that all such planned communities were devoid of vitality. He further asserts, "Jane Jacobs simply couldn't see the ecological disaster the modern city had become," something that Mumford called "willful blindness."[2]

Radburn, New Jersey, another example of 1920s progressive city planning, was designed by Clarence Stein and Henry Wright, the same architects who designed Sunnyside in collaboration with landscape designer Marjorie Sewell Cautley.[3] Dubbed "a city for the motor age," its layout is based on the separation of vehicular and pedestrian traffic. Every home has access to walkways traversing broad stretches of communal green space, so children can run free and neighbors have privacy but do not live in single-lot isolation. Jane obviously thought all contemporary suburbs were terrible, a not unreasonable prejudice when considered as a forecast of urban sprawl. Nevertheless, I felt that there were both good and bad ones and that some planned communities such as Reston, Virginia, which was on the drawing boards at the time I was at Yale, fell into the category of good.

With open-space planning as the subject of my graduate-school thesis, when I moved to New York after my graduation in June 1964, I was imprinted with the ideals of a lifestyle in which human beings either congregate in vibrant community-oriented urban neighborhoods or adopt an anti-suburban sprawl form of home ownership that includes a close association with nature. My choice was to live right in the center of the greatest city in the world. At the same time, I thought it equally important to be in contact with nature and was gratified to learn how green a city New York is in spite of the popular assumption that it is primarily a hardscape of concrete, asphalt, brick, stone, and glass.

With my master's degree from Yale, I could have gotten a job with the New York City Planning Commission, but I correctly surmised that this would give me a professional life more attuned to the kind of master planning I had qualms about than to Jane's principles of neighborhood preservation. For me preservation also included the green urbanism I had studied as a planning paradigm, and I therefore set forth on an environmental advocacy career that included saving the city's parks from further encroachments and its remaining wetlands from garbage dumping.[4]

In proceeding with my activist protests centered on wetlands preservation and reclamation I learned that Robert Moses had been the driving force behind a great deal of dump-cum–future park creation during his tenure as commissioner from 1934 to 1960. His plan for the creation of several new parks was based on converting decommissioned "sanitary landfills," i.e., dumps on wetlands, and capping their top layers of garbage with "clean" soil for the construction of new recreational facilities. Marine Park in Brooklyn and Flushing Meadows Park in Queens (the latter the site of the 1939 and 1964 New York World's Fairs, for both of which Moses had supervised the design and construction) are two examples of former wetlands that he turned into parks.

It's hard to say that Moses's numerous additions to New York City's park system were unwise, but when you think of how marshes serve as spongy barriers and buffers against coastline destruction in times of hurricanes as well as rich breeding grounds for many species of marine life, you have to deplore the fact that *every* piece of New York City marshland, except for a few leftover remnants, has been obliterated by landfill. The plan by James Corner's landscape architectural firm, Field Operations, for the park on the Department of Sanitation's Fresh Kills landfill site is estimated to be realized as a design-guided self-regeneration project over a period of thirty years. The last remaining and largest of the city's former salt marshes, Fresh Kills is still undergoing the release of methane gas from its buried deposits of decaying garbage and will only be opened as a public park incrementally as certain parts have regenerated and become nontoxic.

·

More than the wetlands destruction spearheaded by Robert Moses was at stake. Forested parts of the city were also in peril. At the same time that Jane was spearheading the campaign to bring the construction of the Lower Manhattan Expressway to a halt, I was marching with the Staten Island Citizens Planning Committee to protest the proposed route of the Richmond Parkway, another Robert Moses highway, which was slated to go along the central woodland spine of the island. Bradford Greene, a landscape architect and resident of Staten Island, who had formerly been employed in building the planned community of Greenbelt, Maryland, coined the name Staten Island Greenbelt for the 4.8-mile north–south ridge running most of the length of the borough. Fortunately, the group of Staten Island citizens leading the fight won. Look on a parks map today and you'll see that the Staten Island Greenbelt comprises Reed's Basket Willow Swamp, Willowbrook, and High Rock parks, along with the William T. Davis Wildlife Refuge, Deere Park, and LaTourette Park, which is a golf course with hiking trails through forested areas. As in the case of Jane's triumph over Moses in the battle over the construction of the Lower Manhattan Expressway, saving the Staten Island Greenbelt was a great victory for preserving one of New York's finest remaining natural woodlands.

My further forays into Greater New York City's five boroughs as a park activist in the 1960s took me to such places as Jamaica Bay next to JFK airport, Inwood Hill Park at the northern tip of Manhattan, and Pelham Bay Park in the Bronx. These experiences provided the impetus for writing my first book, *The Forests and Wetlands of New York City,* published in 1971. (I think of my recent book *Green Metropolis* as *The Forests and Wetlands of New York City* redux, since it was born out of a desire to revisit the areas I had written about in the earlier one.)[5] Wishing to know more about the history of the "emerald queen" of New York's system of parks, I published my second book, *Frederick Law Olmsted's New York,* a year after *The Forests and Wetlands.* Because of the dire condition of Olmsted's great masterpiece, it became the catalyst for my twenty-year career in Central Park, first as the leader of a small volunteer organization called the Central Park Task Force and then, after Ed Koch's election as mayor, as the Central Park administrator and founder of the Central Park Conservancy. Another book, *Landscape Design: A Cultural and Architectural History,* published by

Abrams in 2001, six years after I had stepped down as administrator and president of the Conservancy, is the one I call my magnum opus since it was ten years in the making and comprises a broad history of cities, parks, and gardens worldwide.

•

I wish to talk more now about Jane's and my respective ideals about urban life. There is a difference, although certainly not a dichotomy, between our outlooks on what makes cities great. Rereading *The Death and Life of Great American Cities* when I was preparing to give this talk tonight, I felt as if I was in a time machine traveling back half a century. I was struck by the fact that New York City is an entirely different place now than it was when "Mother Jacobs"—Mumford's sexist epithet for her—analyzed the ways in which authoritarian master planning was destroying her concept of neighborhood as the soul of urban life.

Jane was, as I am too, a product of the 1950s. Neither of us could have imagined the tsunami-sized wave of social change that was about to engulf the greatest of great American cities. At the time she published her book in 1961, John Lindsay was a US congressman soon to be elected mayor of New York. As the '60s youth culture reacted to the conservative values of our parents' generation, the decorum of society dissolved and New York City became a very different place from the one it was before. However, being on the whole liberal in their political values, during the era when racial protest against white supremacy resulted in riots in Newark and Detroit, both Black and white New Yorkers, although still nervous about neighborhood safety, lauded Lindsay for walking the streets of Harlem in the turbulent days in 1968 following the death of Martin Luther King.

The Lindsay administration also brought a new approach to urban planning. The talented young architects who prepared a master plan for the entire city—something New York had never had—were different from those of the old Moses-dominated regime. Jane approved of their plan for Battery Park City and felt, as did the Urban Land Institute when it honored the plan with a Global

Award for Excellence in 2010, that it was "a model for successful large-scale planning efforts and [marked] a positive shift away from the urban renewal mindset of the time."

During the same period that this was going on, Lindsay was encountering large labor issues as one after another arm of city government—transit workers, teachers, sanitation workers, and other civil service employees, including those who operated the city's drawbridges and sewage treatment plants—went on strike. By the time he left office, the city was lurching toward economic disaster, and his successor, Abraham Beame, was left to deal with a fiscal crisis as the municipal government was on the brink of defaulting on its bond obligations.

Corporations moved to greener pastures, literally, and with them came the simultaneous flight of the white middle class to the same suburban refuges. Simultaneously, Jane Jacobs–style residential neighborhoods within the city changed dramatically. Opportunistic slumlords rented rundown housing stock to impoverished African American and Puerto Rican immigrants. Because of owners' unpaid municipal real estate taxes and the tenants' frequent lack of utility services and basic security measures, many of these buildings were of necessity vacated by their residents. Some became havens for the homeless, and many in the South Bronx went up in flames due to arson, leaving vast swaths of charred rubble to be carted away by the city to its wetland dumping grounds.

Once-vibrant Harlem became a byword for danger. Crime was rampant, drugs ubiquitous, and robberies and muggings routine. And it wasn't just the poorer neighborhoods like Harlem that suffered. Throughout the city there were garbage-strewn streets, and walking down the sidewalk was a malodorous experience because of ubiquitous curbside dog droppings. The air was a smog of smoke and dust from garbage incinerators. And the parks? If you don't remember, you can certainly imagine.

Who was I to act the role of Pollyanna and think that Central Park should remain a city park instead of being turned over to the federal government and operated as a national park, as Daniel Patrick Moynihan, who was running for his first US Senate term at the time, recommended? Why not subscribe to the suggestion of those who claimed that, since the city was practically broke, the state should take ownership of the park? By this time Jane was living in Toronto, but I am sure that as the paramount champion of city autonomy she would have disapproved of these last-gasp strategies as much as I did. This is when I decided to take off my advocacy hat for good and stop begging for more funds for parks in the dwindling city budget. From me there would be no more Op Ed–style scolding of indifferent government officials. I now realized that it was time to work from inside, rather than outside, New York City's parks department and ignore those who said, "We're taxpayers after all and private citizens shouldn't pay for the upkeep of the parks. That's a city responsibility."

In spite of its danger and decrepitude, Central Park was still used and still loved because of what it had always been: the iconic green heart of the city. Its creation had been a civic enterprise inspired by citizens. Why couldn't a partnership between citizens and government come to its rescue? Fortunately, this is what happened when recently elected Mayor Ed Koch and his newly appointed park commissioner, Gordon Davis, supported my vision. In 1979, Gordon appointed me to the position of Central Park administrator (my city title) and then helped me found the Central Park Conservancy, the organization of which I became director (my private-sector title) the following year. My dual reporting relationship, to the city on one hand and the board of the Conservancy on the other, proved to be a successful model, and other private citizen groups began to form park conservancies not only in New York City but also in other cities throughout the country.

I'd like now to reflect on the dual fact that in the nineteenth century Central Park was a purpose-built people's park and that in the twentieth it was saved by people whose gifts, large and small, enabled a series of restoration projects and new management protocols. I am proud to say here in this historic synagogue that from its earliest days the park's turnaround was made possible by the generosity of Jewish philanthropists who have continually sought to give some of their wealth back to the city where they made their

fortunes. I will say too that it annoys me when some people stigma-
tize the Conservancy as an elitist organization. Their anti-rich-peo-
ple attitude ignores the fact that it is a public–private partnership
supported by New Yorkers of all income levels and diverse walks of
life. Because of their donations, the Conservancy gained the financial means to professionally manage the park that the city budget
could not supply. Beyond this, it would not look the way it does
today without the three hundred volunteers who work alongside the
Conservancy's zone gardeners. As a result, Central Park did not die
and continues to serve as a symbolically important and universally
visible manifestation of American democracy in the public sphere.

.

Here I would like to both agree with and take issue with Jane when,
in chapter 5 of *Death and Life of Great American Cities,* she points
out, "Parks are volatile places. They tend to run to extremes of popularity and unpopularity. . . . They can be delightful features of
city districts, and economic assets to their surroundings as well, but
pitifully few are. They can grow more beloved and valuable with
the years, but pitifully few show this staying power."[6]

If you want to talk about staying power, consider the volunteers
who feel that it is a privilege to be public-space gardeners elsewhere
than Central Park. Sheridan Square and the garden on the site of
the former Women's House of Detention next to the historic Jeffer-
son Market Courthouse are examples not far from where Jane once
lived. Look also at the passion with which community gardeners
throughout the city defend the vacant lots they have claimed and
made into beds of vegetables and flowers, venues for artistic expres-
sion, and sites for Puerto Rican *casitas.*

Good parks for Jane meant a mix of park users—pedestrian
commuters on their way to and from work, mothers and tots at
play in the mid-morning, staff from nearby offices on lunch break,
older children in the afternoon after school. Bad parks were ones
located in the kinds of neighborhoods that used to be called Skid
Row where many of the regular park users were vagrants, alcohol-
ics, and drug addicts, and she concurred with popular opinion in

maintaining that such parks should not be allowed to exist in urban areas associated with "down-and-outers." She also frowned upon siting parks in commercial districts because these locations did not encourage sociable recreational use.

Let me point out one remarkable exception to this bleak perspective. Back in the 1970s, Bryant Park in midtown Manhattan was as forlorn and drug-ridden as Central Park. Laid out as a Beaux-Arts-style public square behind the New York Public Library on Fifth Avenue and 42nd Street, it was a somewhat sinister, shadowy haven for druggies and winos. But it didn't stay that way. At this juncture in our conversation this evening I'd like to welcome the spirit of the late William H. Whyte. Holly, as he was commonly known, was revered for his populist attitude toward cities almost as much as was Jane, and his prescriptive writings about the things that count most in good park-making have been widely accepted. At Bryant Park a brilliant redesign incorporating Holly's public-space sociology was realized in such simple things as open view lines, clean bathrooms, and a flexible seating arrangement by means of movable chairs. Ongoing high-level maintenance beyond what the city could provide was ensured by the creation of a Bryant Park business improvement district (BID), which operates under a contract with the city that authorizes it to administer all aspects of the park's operations. The primary revenue for this comes in the form of assessment fees paid by nearby building owners.

I have one final reservation about Jane's philosophy of what constitutes a good park. Yes, of course vibrant activity counts for a great deal, but there are some parks where it is a relief not to find lots of user attractions. These are places where you can take a nature hike and pretend you are on a trail in the Catskills. One such park is Inwood Hill Park, which you can reach by taking the A Line to its final Manhattan stop. Now turn around and go almost to the other end of the A Line in the Rockaways; get off at Broad Channel in the middle of Jamaica Bay and visit the nature center that is part of Gateway National Recreation Area. There you can hang out with the birders and see several species of waterfowl and nesting osprey. Or drive over the Verrazzano Bridge and go to High Rock on Staten Island, which is where I had what may remain a once-in-my-lifetime experience of watching the emergence of a brood of seventeen-year cicadas.

A particular pleasure for me is the geology lesson I get from my frequent walks in the Ramble in Central Park, where Olmsted and Vaux incorporated into their Greensward plan numerous outcrops and boulders of Manhattan schist. Today I like to see how the Conservancy is enhancing the Ramble's woodland ecology with native plant material.

Here I am sure I am being unfair to Jane. Of course she would applaud today's restored Central Park for its users' ethnic diversity, buskers' impromptu performances on the Mall, ticket lines for Shakespeare on the path leading to the Delacorte Theater next to Turtle Pond, children sledding in the snow on Pilgrim Hill, bird-watchers in the Ramble and North End Ravine, and the sunbathers on the Sheep Meadow. And I believe that, had she not already been so ardently engaged in her own neighborhood preservation cause, she would probably have been an activist in the environmental movement. Indeed, how could she or any of us in this room not appreciate the fact that parks have important nonhuman constituencies, from the annually mating horseshoe crabs in Jamaica Bay to the coyote making a surprise visit to Van Cortlandt Park? I would like to think that tonight we are not only celebrating Jane's great influence on our understanding of the nature of cities but also the diversity of natural life within them and the fact that at this moment in its history, park-rich New York City is enjoying a green golden age.

Notes

New York

1. John Kieran, *A Natural History of New York City: A Personal Report after Fifty Years of Study and Enjoyment of Wildlife within the Boundaries of Greater New York* (Boston: Houghton Mifflin, 1959), 69.

2. *Minutes of the Common Council of the City of New York, 1675–1776*, 8 vols. (New York: Dodd, Mead, 1905), 4:209.

3. Charles Dickens, *American Notes for General Circulation*, 2 vols. (London: Chapman & Hall, 1842), 1:212.

4. Ibid., 1:229.

5. Adriaen van der Donck, "Description of the New-Netherlands" (1653), trans. Jeremiah Johnson, *Collections of the New-York Historical Society*, 2nd ser., vol. 1 (1841), 180.

6. Jasper Danckaerts and Peter Sluyter, *Journal of a Voyage to New-York and a Tour in Several of the American Colonies, in 1679–80*, trans. Henry C. Murphy (Brooklyn, NY: The Long Island Historical Society, 1867), 110.

7. Van der Donck, "Description of the New-Netherlands," 153.

8. Daniel Denton, *A Brief Description of New York, Formerly Called New Netherlands . . .* (1670; New York: W. Gowans, 1845), 3–4.

9. Robert Juet, "The Third Voyage of Master Henry Hudson, toward Nova Zembla . . ." (1611), *Collections of the New-York Historical Society*, vol. 1 (1811), 141.

10. Van der Donck, "Description of the New-Netherlands," 149.

11. Danckaerts and Sluyter, *Journal of a Voyage to New-York*, 136.

12. Denton, *A Brief Description of New York*, 2–3.

13. David Peterson De Vries, "Voyages from Holland to America, A.D. 1632 to 1644," trans. Henry C. Murphy, *Collections of the New-York Historical Society*, 2nd ser., vol. 3 (1857), 110.

14. Danckaerts and Sluyter, *Journal of a Voyage to New-York*, 100.

15. Ibid., 110.

The Hudson River

1. Henry James, *The American Scene* (London: Chapman & Hall, 1907), 147–48.
2. Robert Juet, "The Third Voyage of Master Henry Hudson, toward Nova Zembla. . ." (1611), *Collections of the New-York Historical Society,* vol. 1 (1811), 137, 139.
3. John Lambert, *Travels through Canada, and the United States of North America, in the Years 1806, 1807, and 1808,* 2nd ed., 2 vols. (London: Craddock & Joy, 1813), 2:43.
4. Frances Anne [Kemble] Butler, *Journal,* 2 vols. (Philadelphia: Carey, Lea & Blanchard, 1835), 1:205.
5. Washington Irving, *Wolfert's Roost and Other Papers,* rev. ed. (New York: G. P. Putnam and Son, 1868), 9.
6. Quoted in Parke Godwin, *A Biography of William Cullen Bryant,* 2 vols. (New York: D. Appleton, 1883), 2:367.
7. Cedar Grove, the Thomas Cole house and studio in Catskill, New York, is now a designated National Historic Landmark. As such, it is open to visitors, and its grounds may be visited by the public free of charge from dawn to dusk every day.
8. John K. Howat, *The Hudson River and Its Painters* (New York: Viking, 1972), 45.
9. *Peter Kalm's Travels in North America: The English Version of 1770,* 2 vols. (New York: Wilson-Erickson, 1937), 1:326.
10. Quoted in Pierre M. Irving, *The Life and Letters of Washington Irving,* 3 vols. (New York: G. P. Putnam's Sons, 1869), 1:38–39.

"An American Kew"

1. Andrew Jackson Downing, "Kew Gardens" (1850), in *Rural Essays* (New York: G. P. Putnam, 1853), 486.
2. Ibid., 487, 489.
3. "The New-York Park" (1851), in *Rural Essays,* 150.
4. John Mullaly, *The New Parks beyond the Harlem* (New York: Record & Guide, 1887), title page.
5. Ibid., 63.
6. Ibid., 67–69.
7. "An American Kew," *New York Herald,* March 22, 1891.
8. Nathaniel Lord Britton, *History of the New York Botanical Garden* (Bronx, NY: The Garden, 1915), 1. All reports, plans, board minutes, and correspondence cited in this essay are held in the archives of the New York Botanical Garden, housed in the LuEsther T. Mertz Library.
9. *New York Herald,* "An American Kew."
10. With a partner, John Holbrook, Brinley had set up a private landscape design practice, and although this initial plan is by Holbrook alone, the firm's name, Brinley & Holbrook, appears on several subsequent plans for the Garden's development.
11. Peter Mickulas, *Britton's Botanical Empire: The New York Botanical Garden and American Botany, 1888–1929* (New York: New York Botanical Garden Press, 2007), 79.

12. See "Roses and the New Rose Garden," *Journal of the Horticultural Society of New York* 2.12 (February 1917): 185–86.
13. Britton to F. S. Lee, September 24, 1924.

Green-Wood Cemetery

1. D. B. Douglass, *Exposition of the Plan and Objects of the Green-Wood Cemetery* (New York: Narine, 1839), 12.
2. *Green-Wood Illustrated in Highly Finished Line Engravings by James Smillie . . . with Descriptive Notices by Nehemiah Cleaveland* (New York: Robert Martin, 1847).
3. Nehemiah Cleaveland, *Greenwood: A Directory for Visitors* (New York: Greenwood Cemetery, 1850), 68–84.
4. Cleaveland, *Green-Wood Illustrated,* 90–91.
5. Ibid., 93.
6. Ibid., 23.
7. Andrew Jackson Downing, "Public Cemeteries and Public Gardens" (1851), in *Rural Essays* (New York: Leavitt & Allen, 1853), 155, 157; and "The New-York Park" (1851), ibid., 148–53.

Designing Prospect Park

1. Calvert Vaux to Frederick Law Olmsted, June 3, 1865, in *The Papers of Frederick Law Olmsted* (hereafter *PFLO*), vol. 5, *The California Frontier, 1863–1865,* ed. Victoria Post Ranney (Baltimore: Johns Hopkins University Press, 1990), 387.
2. Olmsted to Vaux, March 12, 1865, ibid., 324–25.
3. Vaux to Olmsted, May 10, 1865, ibid., 359.
4. Olmsted to Vaux, June 8, 1865, ibid., 390.
5. "Preliminary Report to the Commissioners for Laying Out a Park in Brooklyn, New York" (1866), in *PFLO*, supplementary series, vol. 1, *Writings on Public Parks, Parkways, and Park Systems,* ed. Charles E. Beveridge and Carolyn F. Hoffman (Baltimore: Johns Hopkins University Press, 1997), 80–81.
6. Ibid., 87.
7. Ibid., 105.
8. "Report of the Landscape Architects and Superintendents" (1867), in *PFLO,* vol. 6, *The Years of Olmsted, Vaux & Company, 1865–1874,* ed. David Schuyler and Jane Turner Censer (Baltimore: Johns Hopkins University Press, 1992), 157.
9. "Report of the Landscape Architects and Superintendents" (1868), in *Writings on Public Parks, Parkways, and Park Systems,* 112–41, esp. 117–31.
10. In Central Park the four monumental entrance gates designed in 1865 by Richard Morris Hunt were anathema to Olmsted and Vaux, but these were never realized. Other projects that would have been at odds with the Victorian Gothic style of Vaux's architecture were limited to the park's perimeter and did not alter its original character to any appreciable degree. For example, the magnificent neoclassical exedra fronting Fifth Avenue at 70th Street, with Daniel Chester French's fine bronze bust of Hunt and the flanking allegorical figures, one representing Architecture, the other Painting and Sculpture, is invisible from inside

Central Park and in harmony with Thomas Hastings's design of the Frick mansion opposite it. Nor would anyone deny the fact that Augustus Saint-Gaudens's sculpture of General Sherman at Grand Army Plaza facing the park's entrance at 59th Street is the finest equestrian statue in America.

Robert Moses and the Transformation of Central Park
1. Lewis Mumford, "The Sky Line: Artful Blight," *New Yorker,* May 5, 1951, 84–85.
2. "Parking Lot Foes Routed by Moses," *New York Times,* April 25, 1956.
3. "Hartford Gives City a Cafe for Central Park," *New York Times,* March 14, 1960.
4. "Tiffany's Sues to Bar Park Cafe," *New York Times,* June 6, 1960.
5. "Park Cafe Plan Appears Doomed," *New York Times,* February 16, 1966.

Thirty-three New Ways You Can Help Central Park's Renaissance
1. Entry for July 11, 1859, *The Diary of George Templeton Strong,* ed. Allan Nevins and Milton Halsey Thomas, 4 vols. (New York: Macmillan, 1952), 2:455.
2. Founded in 1847, the Academy of Mount St. Vincent was at the time the city's only institute of higher learning for women.

Jane and Me
1. Acolytes who feel attached to their role models in a familial way sometimes feel free to refer to them by first names. Thus in my conversations with fellow Olmstedians—landscape historians or Olmsted park preservationists—he's often just "Fred." Similarly, Jacobs has her circle of admirers who like to call her by her first name.
2. Lewis Mumford, "The Sky Line: Mother Jacobs' Home Remedies," *New Yorker,* December 1, 1962, 167; Robert Kanigel, *Eyes on the Street: The Life of Jane Jacobs* (New York: Knopf, 2016), 217.
3. Like Sunnyside, Radburn is on the National Register of Historic Places.
4. It is shocking to realize that almost all wetlands within the city's once extensive perimeter fringe of biologically rich marshes were converted into "sanitary landfill" sites.
5. *Green Metropolis: The Extraordinary Landscapes of New York City as Nature, History, and Design* was published by Alfred A. Knopf in 2016. I originally thought I would title it *Beyond the End of the Line* since almost all of the parks I wrote about are at the end of subway lines. I realized that this sounded too dour, so I chose *Green Metropolis* as the better title. *Green Metropolis* is not really meant to be a guidebook, but if you are inclined to use it that way, you will find in the back public transportation directions to every park I discuss.
6. Jane Jacobs, *The Death and Life of Great American Cities* (New York: Random House, 1961), 89.

Index